GALLIPOLI
THE WAR NOBODY WON

...AND THE MAN WHOSE LIFE IT STOLE

KENN LORD

LUMINOSITY PUBLISHING LLP

GALLIPOLI
THE WAR NOBODY WON
... AND THE MAN WHOSE LIFE IT STOLE
Copyright © JULY 2020 KENN LORD

ISBN: 978-1-910397-58-9

Cover Art by Poppy Designs
Interior Artwork Kenn Lord

ALL RIGHTS RESERVED

No part of this literary work may be reproduced in any form or by any means, including electronic or photographic reproduction, in whole or in part, without the written permission of the publisher.

TABLE OF CONTENTS

DEDICATION 7
FOREWORD 11
THE MILITARY VETERAN'S HOSPITAL 13

BOOK ONE

PROLOGUE 17
1. THE FIRST GREAT WAR: THE HOW AND WHY OF IT......................19
2. THE WAR THE WORLD HAS TRIED TO FORGET 21
3. ANZAC DAY: TO BE OR NOT TO BE 29
4. CHARLIE'S WORLD: THE SIMPLE LIFE OF A SIMPLE MAN 35
5. THE 5TH LIGHT HORSEMAN: EMU FEATHERS AND SKILL 41
6. THE INDIAN OCEAN AND THE SANDS OF EGYPT 45
7. ANZAC COVE: THE BAD AND THE BEAUTIFUL 49
8. HOW THE WAR STARTED: NOT THE OFFICIAL VERSION 55
9. ANZAC: THE BIRTH OF THE LEGEND..63
10. THE INFAMOUS LANDING: GLORIFIED TRUTH IN PRINT 67
11. CAPE HELLES: IAN HAMILTON STRIKES AGAIN 73
12. THE ANZAC CAMPSITE: NOT THE COVE HILTON 75
13. THE TANGLED WEB OF THE MIDDLE EAST 79
14. THEY HAD TO COME: THE KILLING FIELDS 85
15. GALLIPOLI ACCESSORIES: U-BOATS AND AEROPLANES 94
16. ME GROWING UP 103
17. THE OTHER CHARLIE: THE TIMES THAT MELLOWED HIM 109
18. THE GALLIPOLI SUMMER: TURNING UP THE HEAT 117

19. AT HOME IN ROCKHAMPTON: SINCE THEY WENT AWAY 121
20. THE TRENCHES AT ANZAC COVE: THE LONG-HOT SUMMER .. 125
21. THE WAR ROLLS ON: FROM BAD TO BIZARRE 133
22. THE HOSPITAL SHIPS AND THE ANGELS OF MERCY 149
23. SOMETHING OUT OF THE WRECK: A MOVE TO ACTION? 151
24. THE HOPED-FOR MOVE: DANTE'S INFERNO 161
25. THE PLOT THICKENS: THE CALM BEFORE ANOTHER STORM .. 171
26. OUT OF THE TERRIBLE DARKNESS: A NEW HOPE 181
27. HOW THE MIGHTY FELL: SUVLA BAY: DO OR DIE 189
28. DAD'S LAST GASP: THE BEGINNING OF THE END 201
29. THE END OF MY FATHER'S GALLIPOLI 205
30. GALLIPOLI: THE LAST GOODBYES 209

BOOK TWO

31. GALLIPOLI: THE AFTERMATH 215
32. DAD'S LAST POST 219
33. GALLIPOLI 2015: THE ANZAC COMMEMORATIVE 225
34. THE MAGIC OF ISTANBUL 227
35. THE REAL REASON FOR THE TRIP 231
36. THE ICEMAN COMETH 235
37. LONE PINE IN THE SUN 243
38. LOOKING BACK 245
AUTHOR BIOGRAPHY 247
INDEX OF IMAGES 249
INDEX OF DIARY ENTRIES 251

DEDICATION

EARTHQUAKES OF GRATITUDE TO MY devoted wife Margaret, my daughter Amy, her husband Groover, my son Kelly, his wife Melanie, and my grandkids Gaby, Maddie, and Emelia, all of whom encouraged me through the ten years of disappointment when this book was rejected by most of the influential publishing houses in the world. I was on the verge of giving up when it was picked up by Luminosity Publishing in London. Kate Miles and her gifted production team have brought it wonderfully to life, and in so doing, have given my Father's weeks in the trenches of Gallipoli the acknowledgement, empathy, and respect they deserve. He can now rest in peace.

This book is for my Dad, a gentle man who fought in a killer's world

4:30 A.M. APRIL 25, 2020
EASTERN AUSTRALIAN TIME

IN 2020 AUSTRALIA, TRADITIONAL ANZAC DAY Memorial Events were cancelled due to Covid-19.

Deprived of their chances to attend Dawn Services all over the Eastern Seaboard States of Queensland, New South Wales, Victoria, and Tasmania, Australians from all walks of life were encouraged to bond via the lighting of candles outdoors—and by tuning into simultaneous broadcasts of official services on radio, television, and mobile phones. Public response was overwhelming.

In the soft glow of pre-dawn, seas of lighted candles flickered in domestic driveways, on sidewalks, and in private gardens all over the country. As the sun rose, the nostalgic notes of the "Last Post" played out in the misty stillness of the early morning. There were similar candle tributes in the slightly later time zones of South and Western Australia.

We never forget.

THE MILITARY VETERAN'S HOSPITAL GREENSLOPES, BRISBANE, AUSTRALIA

APRIL 14, 1967

MY FATHER'S WORDS ON THE DAY HE DIED

> *"There was only one law on Gallipoli. Kill or be killed. That was it. It was what we had to do to stay alive. The human values I grew up with, lost a bit more of their meaning every time I loaded a gun or pulled a trigger, and every time I did, a little bit of me died. Every time I saw a mate drop, or I carried one, broken and bleeding, to the casualty shelter on the beach, I prayed that one day I'd be able to understand what I'd had to do."*

BOOK ONE

PROLOGUE

1915. GALLIPOLI—THE MIDDLE EAST. A Blind Tiger on the Loose.

The New Millennium cliché: Gallipoli—a Glorification of War.

Not everyone buys it. They never have. They never can.

Never while the flags of Australia and New Zealand flutter in the wind.

Anzac Day says it all. Lest we Forget.

The day originally honoured the sacrifices of the Gallipoli trenches, the fields of France, and the desert sands of Palestine.

It has vaulted the years to include all wars that involved Australia and New Zealand, the lands of the Southern Cross.

THE ANZAC GENERATION OF 1914-1918 were Destiny's children.

Young men and women, born in Australia and New Zealand, were linked by blood to the British Empire. They lived in countries that gave them their freedom. They had chances. They worked. They owned. They prospered. They had choices. They loved. They married. They bore children. The future was theirs.

Then, in 1914—Britain declared war on Germany.

The threat of losing their freedom if Britain was defeated gave the ANZAC generation pause. They chose to fight in the Empire's name. They have never died.

My Dad was one of them.

At the outbreak of The Great War, he was a twenty-six-year-old jackeroo who lived and worked in Rockhampton, Queensland. He loved his horses, his cattle dogs, and his world. He was a simple happy man.

The apple of his eye was my mother, the girl he wanted to marry.

In December 1914, news of the war came to Rockhampton via the Brisbane Courier that arrived by steam train on the morning after it was published.

The printed word confirmed that the British Empire and its dominions were in trouble. Dad read that as trouble for Rockhampton.

Like thousands of young Aussies, he answered the call to arms.

He became a 5th Light Horseman; Queensland Division, in December 1914.

In the trenches of Gallipoli, he rode the Blind Tiger for 131 days.

He survived and came home.

He married my mother and loved his family, but Gallipoli never left him.

How can it ever leave us?

THE FIRST GREAT WAR: THE HOW AND WHY OF IT

April 15, 1912: The Twentieth Century was young and brave when it was shaken to its core by the North Atlantic death of the *Titanic*.

Two years later, it was shaken again.

The outbreak of the Great War in Europe unleashed its wipeout of the bright promises of the new century. Hopes and dreams went up in flames. Glorious young men and women, nature's gift to the world, would perish; never again to be held in a lover's arms, never to be mothers or fathers; never to smile at a gurgling child.

Western Europe bore the brunt of it when France, Russia and Great Britain stood against the might of industrial Germany.

In December 1914, the sharp claws of war turned on the Middle East.

The Ottoman Empire sided with Germany, and the soldiers of the Turkish army greased their rifles.

Among the fighting men who clashed with them in battle were enlisted men from the Australian and New Zealand Army Corps, who, for reasons of easy identification, became the ANZACS—the legend was born.

THE WAR THE WORLD HAS TRIED TO FORGET

REAMS HAVE BEEN WRITTEN ABOUT Gallipoli; millions of words on hundreds of thousands of pages. It has been talked about, ridiculed, glorified, and damned. It has been dramatised on film and television, recorded, and studied in countless documents, wrapped in sentiment, and spoken about in whispers. Children learn about it in schools. Ordinary men and women have been awed by it. Great men dismiss it.

It was the first war to be imaged in thousands of photographs and newsreels.

Within weeks of the first landings on its beaches, it was making history.

The mention of its name can trigger arguments and enflame the ire of cynics. It has puzzled generations.

Its mistakes are maddening, its intrigue is endless. Gallipoli is forever. Its truth lies in dairies written during the conflict. They are not rare, but we don't always know much about the men who wrote them. We know their names and where they came from. We read their accounts in wonder and awe.

Like hundreds of his mates, Dad kept a diary too, a running story in sequence, day by day for the 131 days he was at Anzac Cove in 1915. He wrote about where he fought, what he saw, what he felt; why he fought, what the war did to him, what it took from him, what it gave him, what it left him with, and how he survived when he thought he never would.

He enlisted. He trained. He sailed away and came home a different man.

He was one of six hundred-and-fifty reinforcements sent into the hell of Anzac Cove two weeks after the first landing on Sunday, April 25, 1915. Six-hundred-and thirty-nine of those men didn't come back. He was one of the eleven who did, and he spent the rest of this life wondering why.

Dad was a first-generation Aussie; a true-blue country bloke who called a spade a shovel, a poser a mug, and a liar a liar. His christened name was Charles James Frewen-Lord, Charlie Lord to his family and mates. If you'd asked him to describe himself, he wouldn't have known where to start.

I do. This book is about him.

The four months he was on Gallipoli seemed like forever; a telling passage of time that grabbed him and held him. Despite the wretched conditions and the mad tug-of-war of the campaign, he stayed committed to his writing because he wanted the people he loved, and those who loved him, to know how it was if he never came home.

"Like I was writing from the grave."

DAYS AFTER MY FATHER DIED, my mother and I read through his diary together. I had never read it, I knew it existed, but he never made a big deal about it, and it was never trotted out as something important. It came alive for me that day. My mother had read it many times with him, words and sentences that were hard to believe.

In reliving them with my mother, Dad eventually came to terms with what happened to him.

In the loneliness of my mother's life after he died, I sat with her through more readings of his diary—therapy for her. She recalled Dad's comments and repeated them to me. I wrote them down, as all writers do, and they are included in this story.

So much has been written about Gallipoli, that it seems impossible to imagine any more can be said, but many of the things that have been written, have branded it as a horror story—better lost and forgotten.

Is that all it was?

Or is there something deeper? Something intangible, something so touching that it continues to live on, despite efforts that encourage us to forget it.

Charlie's diary records what he experienced from his limited point of view in and around the front-line trenches above Anzac Cove, up and down the rocky rises close to the beach. He details his part in the battles that involved his regiment, every detail set against the dazzling blue of the Aegean Sea in Gallipoli's late spring and summer of 1915.

His diary is not a history book. He was an observer, not a historian.

His shocks are not carefully planned; they come out of nowhere and hit with a wallop. His no-frills revelations confirm that after years of intense scrutiny, Gallipoli is still the brain-scrambler it always was.

Contradictions are the norm. There are shadows and dark corners—cover-ups, skulduggery, wrong turns, ego demons, dodgy happenings, and creaky doors. Nothing is cut and dried.

Gallipoli is Alfred Hitchcock, Agatha Christie, and Shakespeare. It is Barnum & Bailey, Grand Opera, and The Greatest Show on Earth.

It does not play rules. *Dad called it a Blind Tiger.*

Whenever he told me things about the war, he never referred to the Turks as the bad guys. He saw them as the enemy and knew too well that they saw him as the enemy.

"Nothing personal; it was simple arithmetic."

My young friends could never understand that. They wanted Dad to be Robin Hood, and the Turks to be the Sheriff of Nottingham. They were even more slack-jawed when Dad called Gallipoli beautiful. He had no trouble looking beyond the carnage to admire it.

The Peninsula's eastern seaboard, facing the Aegean Sea, is especially enchanting. The Straits of the Dardanelles, on the western seaboard, are breathtaking. Today, it's impossible to believe what happened there.

Gallipoli holds the Australia and New Zealand of 1915, in its arms; it is part of us because it is part of the men and women whose lives it stole or touched. Few of us in today's world can fully imagine what really went down in that long-ago summer, but while imagining cannot paint a clear picture, there is something indefinable that can, and whatever it is, it is powerful enough to draw millions of us to Dawn Services on Anzac Day every year, potent enough to keep us still as the sun rises on those mornings, real enough to make us think; emotional enough to bring tears to the eyes of all kinds of people when the bugler plays the "Last Post," the telling moment of every Dawn Service.

In the minds of those who look beyond the horrors, Gallipoli's spirit is filled with wisdom and insight. It gives majesty to death, holds dear the unending dedication of nurses on the hospital ships, and the souls of the gallant young men and boys who fought insane battles on the bloody fields of hell.

Compare Gallipoli to the American Civil War; a clash of beliefs; North against South; belief challenging belief: soldiers on each side driven by belief.

On Gallipoli, there was none of that. It was Empire against Empire; might against might, and the soldiers on each side were means to an end.

The ridiculous part is that after all the bloodshed, nobody won. That whole campaign was so messed up, that even those who served in it didn't know what was going on. There was always too much happening and not nearly enough of the right things happening.

The ANZACs were particularly stumped by the politics of the conflict and the often-baffling decisions of the military powerbrokers in Great Britain.

My father referred to them as: "*The London High Command.*" The correct title was "The Dardanelles Committee" or as one of Dad's mates called them: "Georgie's Boys," a reference to David Lloyd George, the Brit Munitions Minister who is widely credited for kick-starting the Middle East power games in the first place. Whether he did or didn't, doesn't matter.

This story is not about him, but if you've got to have a sorcerer, a shady puppet master who pulled the strings, he could be the man.

Like other kids my age, I learned about the Dardanelles Campaign in history class at school. I had the advantage of my father's first-hand knowledge, and when I came home with questions, his answers were not always the same as those in the books we were reading.

He'd shake his head and say, "*I can only tell you what I know.*"

Charlie did not consider himself an authority on that campaign. Has there ever been any one person anywhere, on either side of the fight, who could pin exactly went wrong, without bias and without making excuses?

For most of Dad's time on Gallipoli, he was confined in Anzac Cove, but he was close to the word-of-mouth grapevine that carried news of the battles elsewhere on the Peninsula, and he was familiar enough with the overall picture to pass comment and draw his own conclusions. I base my conclusions on his answers to questions I brought home from school; to conversations he had with visitors to our house, and to comments passed on to me by my mother. *None of that makes me an authority either.*

You are reading my father's version of the story, an expanded take on what he wrote in his diary while the ever-changing mess was going on around him.

He was no diarist; he didn't have one at home; a diary was an exception for him. He rarely wrote anything down; he never wrote letters. He said he was "*rotten at English*" and it irked him that he couldn't always write what he felt. He said he didn't have "*enough words*" and that composing sentences "*took too much bloody time.*" All I can say is, the school he attended way out west must have had one hell of a teacher. Dad hasn't done too badly for a kid who was "*rotten at English and doesn't have enough words.*"

Luckily, he was blessed with a great memory for detail. It was one of his gifts, which is why I'm puzzled that some of his diary dates don't match up with official records.

The Anzac Cove summer of 1915 was etched on pages in his mind; he could call them up and speak them at the drop of a hat. He was not always anxious to do that, but when I was growing up, he thought I should know something about the war he fought. He didn't tell me everything, I was just a kid, but what he did tell me was enough to make me understand what happened to Gary Cooper in *For Whom the Bell Tolls*.

Gallipoli was, and is, juicy fodder for Australia's anti-Brit peddlers who love getting stuck into it for "*letting the side down,* for *putting the Empire above human life,*" and for throwing young Aussies "*to the snapping dogs of war.*" After listening to Dad's stories, I knew what the critics were on about. Gallipoli confuses people.

It confused Dad, and he was there.

PAGES FROM DAD'S DIARY

ANZAC DAY:
TO BE OR NOT TO BE

STAFF SERGEANT C J LORD; NO 291, did not die on Gallipoli; neither did Gallipoli die in him. It lived on in the dark canyons of his mind for fifty-three years, and it was with him at the end. He passed on in Greenslopes Hospital in Brisbane at the age of seventy-nine in April 1967, just days before Anzac Day.

Since 1916, the date of April 25 has been notable in Australia, initially to commemorate the first landings of Australian and New Zealand fighting men on Gallipoli, and later to honour those who served our countries in other wars. After the Australian Government declared April 25 a national holiday in 1927, it continued as such through the thirties, forties, fifties, and well into the sixties and seventies. Hotels, retail outlets, places of business and entertainment were closed for all or most of the day. Anzac Day marches drew crowds everywhere; kids waved flags, their oldies reflected, cheered, or wept.

Wreaths and flowers were laid on monuments with honour rolls and statues of men in World War One battle dress in every city, town, and village on the continent and in New Zealand. Those monuments are still there, mounted in prominent places; dutifully maintained and cared for. Anzac Day was as big as it gets. Then, suddenly in the sixties, things changed. Something went wrong.

The "something" was the Vietnam War.

During my father's failing years, young Australian men were being conscripted into National Service and sent to fight in Vietnam. There were protests on the streets of this country. Australia's involvement in that war, fiercely attacked on moral grounds, became an issue that divided public opinion and undermined friendships. The questioning sixties had flown in on the wings of dope. It was the decade of the Flower People, of "Blowin' in the Wind" and Peter, Paul and Mary. John Denver, Bob Dylan, and Jimmy Webb wrote the songs. Woodstock was the gig, San Francisco was the city. *Peace* was the word. Pot was the rage: *Got a problem? Smoke a joint.*

It was no time to be hanging garlands on war heroes, reliving legendary battles, or cheering gutsy survivors. American soldiers on R&R in Sydney were booking into top hotels and cutting it up in King's Cross. So was everyone else; that's what you did in King's Cross, but when battle-weary soldiers were letting off steam in Sydney, Vietnam got the blame, the good-time girls got lucky, and Anzac Day caught the backlash.

Indignant rabble-rousers reached for their paddles and stirred the pot. The loudest tore into the Gallipoli campaign:

> *A monument to the horrors of some disastrous minor skirmish; as useless and politically corrupt as Vietnam; so what's with a public holiday to commemorate a stupid fucking war like that?*

It all sounded profound; especially when it was bellowed on waves of fake emotion! Inevitably, Talkback Radio got on board. It had to happen. Talkback was a giant in the sixties and seventies. There was no internet. No Facebook. No Twitter. Television had news and current affairs but if you were serious about wanting to be "informed" there were high-circulation newspapers and magazines—*Time, Newsweek*, and *The Bulletin.*

But on the airwaves, Talkback was where it all happened, urgent, loud, and irresistible, the live-to-air domain of motor-mouthed hosts who pulled no punches and took no prisoners.

Deliberately fiery, judgemental, and aggressive; they were the unseen vigilantes who influenced public opinion with all the drum-banging they could bring on. They were "The Force" and they harnessed it to feed greedy ears with daily caterwauling that covered the spectrum; if it was out there, it was fodder for the frenzy:

> *Tickets to see Liberace, Glen Campbell, and Shirley Bassey: What a rip-off!*
>
> *Liz Taylor in "Virginia Wolf": She looks like a bag lady!*
>
> *The ineptness of politicians: Send in the Clowns!*
>
> *The unfinished Sydney Opera House: Utzon's folly.*

People listened to this stuff and lapped it up. Talkback could kill a movie, do the same to a restaurant, and question the right of a Queen to sit on a throne!

The up-front Talkback Code:

> *We're fearless! We tell it like it is! Don't take a breath! Don't give 'em a minute to think or a second to disagree. Don't ever shut up, Silence is a killer!*

The backdoor Talkback Code:

> *Muckraking rates! It keeps the advertising bucks rolling in. Keep the birdcages rattling. Keep talking. Keep it juicy. Attack sacred cows! Never let up!*

The loudest muckraking was the gaudy ranting about the Vietnam War and as that war degenerated into the madness and tragedy of political disarray, the louder and more impassioned the Talkback rants became.

> *Why is Australia supporting a senseless campaign that is being fought to pacify America's fear of communism and to big-note Bobby Kennedy?*
>
> *Why are our young men conscripted to fight a fight that isn't ours?*
>
> *How long will this go on: how many more lives will be lost?*
>
> *Why are we behaving like puppets of the God-almighty US of A?*
>
> *Bingo! There go the phones!*

Predictably, Talkback picked up on the most combustible question:

> *Why are we glorifying the horrors of war by celebrating Anzac Day?*

The listening hordes: ears burning, and brains blistered, were fired up: Talkback ratings hit the stratosphere.

In rolled the ads! The Vietnam War was solid gold; a hot topic at weekend barbecues, in hotel dining rooms, on suburban trains and trams, in the fast-food halls of the new wave shopping towns, in city parks and squares, and in the public bars of rowdy pubs: Over-heated pros and cons. Loud noises and empty talk.

Vietnam and Anzac Day: *The Dynamic Duo*. Vietnam: *Napalm and outrage . . .* Anzac Day: *Old Guys with medals*

There was no such thing as fake news in the sixties. Everything reported in the media was gospel! Then the unthinkable happened: A few Returned Service League Clubs, whipped into action by the rants of the ravers, banned Vietnam veterans from membership! Waves of pros and cons roared onto the Talkback airwaves and kept the war forums aloft. More talk! More divided opinions! More hype! More riotous protests in parks with pot and posters:

> *Up the revolution! Roll the cameras. Rant and rave and get your face on telly!*

People stopped and wondered: Was there a truth buried somewhere in all this noise? All too suddenly Anzac marches, eclipsed by the Vietnam thunder, lost their hold on the big crowds of yore. Dawn Services followed suit:

> *Anzac Day? You're joking, mate! They close the pubs!*

My father shook his head. He was disgusted by the decision of RSL Clubs that cold-shouldered Vietnam veterans and said so.

It couldn't last and didn't: When Vietnam turned into a political puzzle that became a too-hot potato, nobody in the country knew enough about the political truth to peel it. When more than one commentator pointed out that the Vietnam War posed no threat to Australia, it soon fell from Talkback fervour, and Anzac Day took its first steps on the slow road to a comeback.

The all-day and part-day closing rules were modified to give the day more freedom, but it had never lost the reverence of those who respected it.

Dad knew that would happen. He had no time for the Talkback Circus, and he was never swayed by party rhetoric or loosely informed social analysing:

> *"Bottle-talk—gone and forgotten when the bottles are empty."*

He was never a bar fly, but he could hone in on bar-fly buzz with his eyes shut.

Through all this nonsense, Anzac Day was always sacred in our house, the *"One Day of the Year"* that Alan Seymour wrote about in his play which used to be performed a lot, now hardly ever is probably because of its negative undertones.

When I was growing up, I went to the Dawn Service with Dad every year. His treasured medals had been polished the night before; he dressed in his best suit, a starched white shirt, and a striped tie. His shoes were buffed, his medals gleamed on the breast of his coat, and his grey felt hat sat straight on his head. On the way to the service, he didn't talk at all.

As the rising sun's rays slowly lit those mornings, I saw the sure signs of what he was feeling when the bugler played the "Last Post." I felt the trembling of his hand in mine and heard the catch of his breath as he fought to keep his breathing even. I stood closer to him then, and felt his trembling hand leave mine to wrap around my shoulder, pulling me closer.

We were not alone. All around us the same things were happening to other families in the almost holy silence, broken only by the soul-stirring sound of that lonely bugle.

There were lots of Gallipoli survivors back then, and they were all haunted by the same memories. As the bugle crystalized those memories, women wept, and girls and boys like me, the sons and daughters of the men who came back, were learning that life was not all cricket bats and doll's houses and Christmas Eve. We learned too, that whatever had happened across the world on that craggy but eerily beautiful peninsula in Turkey was powerful enough to change lives forever.

CHARLIE'S WORLD:
THE SIMPLE LIFE OF A SIMPLE MAN

BEFORE YOU READ THE ENTRIES in Dad's diary it's important for you to meet him; to see him as the dinkum Aussie bloke he was proud to be; to know about the kind of world he lived in, the things that influenced his thinking; the times that patterned his life and cut the cloth of his being.

Charles James Frewen-Lord grew to manhood in the early years of the Twentieth Century. Despite the fancy hyphenated handle, he was plain old Charlie Lord to the people who knew him. He loved animals, had an affinity with horses, and didn't want to be rich or important.

He was not a man of the world and he believed that the people and things that were his life would always be there. As a horseman and a jackaroo, he watched over the cattle in his care; rounded them up with his blue cattle dogs and brought them home. In the winter, he slept out at round-up time, cooked damper in a camp oven, covered his horse and slept beside an open fire.

He covered the camp-oven coals and laid a blanket over the warm soil for the cattle dogs he'd trained and cared for. They were his mates and he treated them like the princes he thought they were.

He met a woman he fell in love with, and he loved her for the rest of his life. They understood each other and truly believed they'd be together until they grew too old to dream. In 1914 my father's place of work was a grazing property in Queen's Park, North Rockhampton. He came from a big family; there were lots of brothers and sisters; his father was dead; his mother a widow. He and my mother were "going together." "Making it legal" was on the agenda. They had met in the Queensland town of Barcaldine when my father, the dashing jackaroo, was working there. My mother's name was Catherine Pontifax; a lovely gentle young woman with a fresh complexion and long dark hair she wore wound up in a bun. She'd had an unhappy life, indifferently treated by a Cinderella stepmother who gave her no affection. She was sustained by the strength of her two sisters and a strong brother, and when she decided to leave her father's house, she found work as a domestic with a family that treated her with respect and stayed close for years.

The name Pontifax was an awkward mouthful in rural Australia; it was changed to Price, and Catherine became Kitty. And so, Charles James Frewen-Lord and Catherine Pontifax, who could have lived on the pages of *Pride and Prejudice,* became Charlie Lord and Kitty Price, more likely to be found hanging out in front of the pickle factory in *The Sentimental Bloke*. Their new Aussie names were much more suited to the town they lived in.

The Rockhampton of 1914, the place my mother and father called home was a handsome central Queensland country town on the banks of the Fitzroy River. It was their world; it fed them; sustained them and made them happy. It was the only world they knew—it harboured them, comforted them, and became part of them. They talked about it to me, and I saw it through their eyes as a clean uncluttered town with wide streets and beautiful Victorian buildings, many of which are still there.

Rockhampton was and still is, a Queensland seaboard town of note. It straddles the Tropic of Capricorn, linked by an invisible line to the western towns of Emerald and Longreach. Just over twenty miles to the east lie the sunny seaside townships of Yeppoon and Emu Park. Due west are the cattle towns of Barcaldine and Blackall.

Rockhampton will always be "Rocky" to dinkum Aussies. It had a forward-thinking local government that laced its main streets with passenger tramlines in 1909. My mother told me she thought its steam-driven trams looked something like the trolley car Judy Garland rode in *Meet Me in St. Louis*.

I think Mum may have been a bit fanciful; I've never thought Rocky or anything in it, looked like Hollywood.

> *"It sounds silly today, but Rocky was our world back then. It was all we knew and all we wanted. We had our friends and we were all close. We were there to help if things went wrong. It's hard to put into words but everything was the way we thought it was supposed to be, and when I look back, I think we were right."*

Here is early Twentieth Century Rockhampton as seen through the eyes of my Mum and Dad: It was sustained by its meatworks, and while it may not have been the commercial hub of the state of Queensland, it was no shantytown. Its importance was boosted by a rail connection to Brisbane in 1903. *Miraculous news!* You could catch a train to Brisbane; from there you could catch a train to Sydney, and from there you could hop a boat to the world!

The Rocky of 1914 was going places, but it was still comfortable and easy-going, with warm summers and even warmer people-next-door.

Its streets were filled with horses and sulkies and riders on bikes; its gardens were filled with flowers; its schools were filled with healthy kids. Its lifestyle was a daily parade of rituals and easy-going-dos-and-don'ts:

The milkman came in the morning and filled the family billycan with fresh warm milk from a ten-gallon can. The milk was chilled in an ice chest on the back verandah where it was cool; a hand-driven separator separated the cream from the milk, *and everyone fought for the cream*. The baker came with bread in a basket covered with a clean white cloth; *point to what you want*. On special days, he came with cream buns and meat pies with peas.

Mum told me she could smell him coming!

The postman came with the mail and always blew a whistle. Huge corrugated iron tanks, sitting on wooden stands held the filtered rainwater. Thousands of chooks laid eggs every day. Roosters crowed in the morning. Dogs barked at the postman. Mango trees grew everywhere, and in December when the mangoes were ripe, kids climbed the trees to raid the fruit, came down with deep yellow mouths, chucked skins and seeds all over the ground, and got donged for doing it.

Rocky menus were simple: three meals a day—breakfast, dinner, and tea! The food was fresh and nutritious: Rolled oats with fresh milk, a dollop of cream and a teaspoon of Millaquin syrup from Bundaberg; home-made Aberdeen sausage, corned beef fritters, cold sirloin salads, rump steaks, apple pies, egg custards, beef stews, meat pies with mashed potatoes and home-grown vegetables, sponge cakes, scones with rosella jam, pikelets with gooseberry jam, rhubarb pies, scallops from the Burnett River, fresh fish from the sea and giant mud crabs from Gladstone: *It was referred to as "proper tucker," mate*

The Sunday Roast was a banquet at a linen-covered table with bread and butter pudding and home-made ginger beer. Summer Sunday afternoons were for lying back in a squatters' chair on the veranda while a cool breeze blew up from the Fitzroy River.

Everyone knew everyone, and everyone cared about everyone else. Peyton Place it wasn't. Rocky was a rural Queensland Utopia; small and funny and fine, *and as far away from Gallipoli as a thousand lovely things could carry it.*

And just a tad isolated:

The world was not the information hotline it has become. Rockhampton's main source of worldwide news came via the *Brisbane Courier* delivered by rail the day after it was printed, and there were two local newspapers, *The Rockhampton Bulletin* and *The Daily Record.* The news that came early in 1914 was not good. The winds of war that had been blowing across Europe for months threatened to erupt into a mortal storm. The powers of the northern hemisphere watched and waited; it was too late for prayers; it would soon be too late for tears.

When war finally broke out, the newspapers told the story. Great Britain, France and Russia stood against the military might of Germany.

In October, Turkey entered the war on Germany's side. This was no domestic shoot-out; this was the Big One, the war to end all wars—the predicted Apocalypse, the Armageddon, the World against the World.

In Great Britain, a desperate call went out to its dominions for assistance.

King George V and Queen Mary had been on the throne for four years. They were the figureheads of the Empire; they were popular; they lived in London, a city in a far-away world with castles and crowns and priceless splendour.

So stood the Empire in the eyes of Kiwis and Aussies, ordinary people who lived ordinary lives. If Great Britain went down, its dominions would go down too. There would be no more "*Mother Country*;" no more "*Land of Hope and Glory.*" In its place was the fear of German or Turkish dominance. Newspapers continued to splash worrying news all over their front pages; the Bad Guys were serious. Britain's call for assistance was answered. Tens of thousands of young Australian men lined up to enlist.

Dad talked it all over with his jackaroo mates in Barcaldine and Blackall, the smaller towns on his round-up runs. Adrenalin-driven excitement smiled at a few of the wilder boys and the beckoning face of a thrilling war smiled back. For them, it seemed a grand adventure dressed in khaki uniforms with brass buttons and broad-brimmed hats with one side turned up.

It's all Rudyard Kipling, chaps!

Dad was not reckless enough to be one of the adventurers; instead, he spoke quietly to my mother about his feelings. Mum told me he talked for ages, puffing on roll-your-owns, and weighing up the situation. He finally based his decision on what he thought could happen if the war ever reached the shores of Australia, and as my mother told it, and told it as often as I had birthdays, this is the essence of what came out:

> *"No bunch of bullies, no matter how big they are, have the right to take anything that belongs to anyone else. No bastards can do that! If they do it 'over there' it won't be long before they'll want to do it here, and if they're big enough they'll try."*

A simple philosophy expressed in simple words by a simple young country bloke who believed it was why he had to fight. No highfalutin sermons from anybody. No outside influences. No stirring talk of duty and honour. No fake patriotism. He put his life on the line for the things and people he loved, and he did it with his heart. I watched him grow old, and he was never belittled by hate or regret. Time beat him in the end as it always beats everyone. It was the only thing that did, but there were times when the Gallipoli trenches came close.

THE 5TH LIGHT HORSEMAN: EMU FEATHERS AND SKILL

THE 5TH LIGHT HORSE WAS A Regiment of Queenslanders formed in Brisbane in the late August and early September of 1914. After registering for enlistment with his mates in Blackall in October, Charlie Lord took care of his affairs in Rockhampton, said goodbye to Kitty Price, caught the train to Brisbane and was officially accepted as a 5th Light Horseman on Tuesday, December 8, 1914. The Light Horse didn't just take anybody.

Enlisting men had to pass a tough test to demonstrate mastery of the horses they rode, and their horses were not just any old horses. They were a special breed with a rogue streak; mostly seeded in the northern fields of rural New South Wales. In country speak they were Walers, often spelled with a small "w." *Not in this book.*

They were owned by the government; assigned as needed. If an enlisted man owned a horse that could measure up, it was bought and paid for.

In Brisbane, my father met his Waler, "*a bit of a brumby but we liked each other.*" The Light Horsemen went into training on the fields of the Army Barracks in the outer Brisbane suburb of Enoggera. There began the bonding of man and horse; unique associations that bred mutual trust.

The distinguishing emblem on the slouch hats worn by the Light Horsemen of Queensland, was a plume of emu feathers attached to the turned-up brim, a flashy adornment first worn by mounted infantrymen who patrolled the streets of the southern Queensland town of Gympie during the Shearer's Strike of the late Nineteenth Century.

Plumed hats and helmets on fighting men were not new; they had been worn for centuries, but the fluffy brown feathers of the Aussie emu perfectly matched the khaki of Aussie uniforms and added a flourish to the otherwise drabness of the battledress. The look was so right that emu feathers were soon adopted by other regiments of the Light Horse.

Dad was proud and said so.

> *"We scored a first, and with bloody emu feathers! We'd been picking them up all over the bush for years."*

But this was no time to be looking in mirrors, polishing buttons or preening in emu-feathered hats on horseback. On the other side of the world, the mortal storm had erupted, and the guns of war boomed louder.

Ready or not, Australia's band of enlisted young men: fighters, adventurers, soldiers, deep-thinkers, lovers, fathers, boyfriends, and mounted horsemen were in demand. The 5th Light Horse left Brisbane by train on Saturday, December 12, arriving in Sydney early on Monday, December 14 to join the Sixth and Seventh Light Horse at Liverpool, where those regiments had been in training.

As Dad told it, Christmas in Sydney was coming in on a bleak note, familiar goodwill was hard to find, and the word "merry" was dying on people's lips.

The big city's seasonal cheer wore an anxious edge. While the flags of Great Britain and Australia fluttered in the wind over her streets, the darkest New Year ever was on its way. The government, conscious of its responsibility towards public morale, made a stout effort to remain close-mouthed about troop movements, but when word got out that the Light Horse Regiments were going to war, waiting crowds lined Sydney's famous harbour to say goodbye.

On Monday, December 21, four days before Christmas, my father and his Waler, along with the rest of his regiment, boarded the *Persic* to sail across the harbour, out of Sydney Heads and across the Great Australian Bight to Albany in Western Australia, then into the Indian Ocean with a convoy of sixteen ships bound for the training sands of Egypt.

> In Dad's words, *"The Harbour Bridge wasn't there then, but there were people everywhere, all over the Domain and Darling Point. There wasn't a lot of noise. People clapped and there were cheer groups and sailboats with flags and whistles. I remember looking back when we sailed through the heads because I didn't know if I'd ever see Sydney again."*

The *Sydney Morning Herald* told it like this:

> *"There was silence on the shores of the harbour as the Persic sailed away: Women waved lavender-scented handkerchiefs moist with tears, and serious people stood thoughtfully still in the summer sun. They watched the departing ship as it crossed the harbour, their steady eyes holding it until it was out of sight. Australia's young men were leaving to fight a war in a faraway world that most of them had never seen. Too many of them will never come home."*

At home in Rockhampton, it was the first time in their relationship that my mother and father had been separated. Like thousands of Aussie mothers, wives, sisters and sweethearts, Kitty Price became one of the women who waited out the war holding tight to the warmth of a yesterday sunshine that may never come again.

THE INDIAN OCEAN AND THE SANDS OF EGYPT

THE VOYAGE TO EGYPT WAS no joyride. The Walers were held below decks; carefully tethered to remain stable with the rolling of the ship in the ocean swell. There they were cared for: brushed, sponged down and exercised in tight quarters that had to be thoroughly cleaned and disinfected every day. One man and seven horses didn't finish the trip and were buried at sea.

The rogue adventurers on board began to have second thoughts, but the Aussie ability to see the lighter side of heavy, kept the men on the *Persic* in good spirits.

On Monday, February 1, 1915, after seven weeks at sea, the *Persic* sailed out of the Suez Canal into the Mediterranean Sea and docked at Alexandria, the exotic seaport of Egypt.

The 5th Light Horsemen disembarked and travelled by train with their horses to Cairo, then transferred to the rail link to Maadi, the site of the British Military Training Camps, twelve miles south, on the east bank of the Nile. After six confined weeks at sea, it was considered unwise for the Walers to be mounted; instead, they were led to Maadi on foot where they quickly acclimatised and settled into the business of training.

All through February March and April; day after day, the training continued: men and horses bonding together; toughening and perfecting the skills of mounted combat. The 5th Light Horse was not the only "*Down Under*" regiment on training detail in Egypt.

The desert was alive and hopping with good-natured Kiwis, Aussies, and Brits, and they were not exactly invisible. There are stories about rabble-rousing Aussie soldiers kicking up in Cairo; heaps of accounts of drinking, reckless behaviour and whoring with Cairo girls.

I didn't ask Dad about that and he didn't volunteer any information. It was never mentioned but he was a healthy virile country jackaroo, and I assume he had healthy urges. I can't say anything more, except that Dad's training time in Egypt was happy.

He developed an affinity with the country and a sentimental attachment to the desert that never waned. He was no real movie buff, but he had his favourite films; all of them about the romance and fantasy of the desert: Gary Cooper in *Beau Geste,* Zoltan Korda's *The Four Feathers* and *The Thief of Bagdad,* the original *Desert Song,* the Aussie classic, *Forty Thousand Horsemen,* and the campy soufflés of the forties pin-up queen, Maria Montez: *Arabian Nights, Ali Baba and the Forty Thieves* and *Sudan.* Maria Montez? *Yes*: Dad had this thing about the desert and I'm sure it had to do with his time in Egypt.

I don't think it had too much to do with the exotic Maria Montez. I didn't ask and he didn't say but when she died, tragically, in a weight-reducing bath in 1951, he was quietly sad.

The Egyptians on duty at Maadi were referred to as "Gyppos" in Aussie speak. They took to the larrikin attitudes of the 5th Light Horsemen and the training ripped along. One of the Gyppos, a happy bouncing trainer named Ali, latched on to the word "Digger," the nickname the men had for each other. Ali had trouble with the pronunciation of Digger; it came out "Drigger."

It amused my father so much that he laid the nickname on me when I was a kid. He never called me anything else; not at home; not anywhere. My name was *Drigger,* even when I copped it for getting into trouble, and even when I was old enough to be Ken or Kenneth or Kenny. *Kenny? Sorry.*

The training went on in a kind of holiday atmosphere: swimming the Walers in the waters of the Nile; *mind the crocs,* and checking out the pyramids across the river by the light of a million stars in a clear night sky. The Great War was yet to show its face to the 5th Light Horse, but as the month of April neared its end, a change was coming in on a fearful north wind that blew in, without warning, from the Aegean Sea.

Other regiments of Australian and New Zealand infantry and Light Horsemen in-training had already been sent from Egypt to Gallipoli to take part in the first landings on April 25. When word reached the High Command in London that those landings had not gone as expected, hasty moves were made to get things back on track. It was always assumed that the 5th Light Horse would sail from Egypt to the battlefields of The Western Front in France. Instead, the decision was made to despatch the 5th to Gallipoli as reinforcements for the first wave of ANZACs. The news was a sledgehammer. Men who had enlisted as mounted horsemen had trained as a man-horse unit, moving and thinking together, each day working towards the ultimate perfection of the partnership.

Suddenly, the men were on infantry detail to be sent into battle *without their horses!* The move triggered furrowed brows, shaking heads, and worried words from the Gyppos in Maadi.

This comment came from one of the Maadi master trainers:

> *"Just like sending hundreds of Davids without their slings and stones to fight the Ottoman Goliaths in fields of their own."*

Nevertheless, the 5th Light Horse went to war; and their hardy Walers remained behind in the lonely safety of the Egyptian desert. When Dad said goodbye to his Waler, a dismayed Ali shook his hand and said, *"We'll be here when you come back."* It was spoken with heavy hope, and Dad got the message:

Ali knew Gallipoli well, and he knew the 5th Light Horse had not been trained for it.

ANZAC COVE:
THE BAD AND THE BEAUTIFUL

HERE BEGINS THE GALLIPOLI MY father was destined to know; one man's account of what it was like to live through 131 days of the infamous campaign that has earned its special place in our country's history.

I have linked his diary entries in sequence to accounts of the politics of the war; his daily life at the Cove; his revelations of the conditions that made existence a near impossibility, and to other events that were to affect what was happening to him and his mates.

To keep the story running I have woven this information into threads of the campaign that streamed across the hills, valleys, and shores of the Gallipoli Peninsula, trapping men on both sides of the conflict, and enmeshing them in battles of unbelievable violence. Reports of what happened on Gallipoli may well be over-familiar and many-sided, but they're necessary here to keep Dad's words relevant. Without them, his diary is an incomplete essay. Like everyone else in this war—soldiers, sailors, nurses, officers, and correspondents, he was too often confused about what was going on.

MAY 5, 1915

Left Maadi today for the Dardanelles.

Arrived at Alexandria after being all night in the train and embarked aboard a captured German boat, the Lutzow.

This diary entry date (above) conflicts with histories of the 5th Light Horse that set the date for the Maadi departure as May 15, not May 5—an easy slip? This is not an unusual occurrence in accounts of the Dardanelles Campaign.

Military communication was anything but efficient. The campaign was a censorship nightmare, but you'd expect a history of the 5th Light Horse to be accurate in every detail.

Suppose the date of May 15 had been officially recorded, perhaps by mistake, in documents that had put the figure one in front of the figure five and it was never challenged. If Dad's date is incorrect, what happened to his ten lost days? Other accounts list the 5th Light Horsemen as landing at Anzac Cove on May 12 to *fight as infantry without their horses.*

I accept that my father wrote everything as it happened, and I therefore, assume that his dates and facts are correct because he was there. He says he left Maadi on May 5, and I accept that; if I don't, the dates of the daily entries that follow must be conspicuously out of place, and I fail to see how they can be.

MAY 6

We sailed for Gallipoli at half past four this morning: I was on submarine duty. The boat was very dirty. We are sailing with all lights out and a destroyer escort: 4th; 5th; 6th; 7th and 10th Light Horse on board: Very crowded.

MAY 7

At sea, nothing eventful occurred. Today we passed some islands and expect to reach the Dardanelles tonight: All going well.

MAY 8

Arrived at Cape Helles during the night and got our first sight of the war.

The flashes of the guns could be plainly seen, and the rifle fire was terrific.

We were anchored all night about two miles out, and left about two o'clock next day for Gaba Tepe, thirteen miles north of Cape Helles.

The first Australians had landed there almost two weeks before and they were fighting the Turks. On the way to Gaba Tepe just before four o'clock in the afternoon, we saw the Queen Elizabeth anchored about four miles out.

Destroyers came alongside to take us off the Lutzow. I went on the destroyer Rattlesnake and arrived on shore near Gaba Tepe at five o'clock.

I had a little rest till all the regiment arrived and went straight up to the trenches. We got shelled going up and lost fifteen men with more wounded.

The killed and wounded were taken down to the Dressing Station near the beach. The Turkish trenches were facing the sea only twenty-five yards away from our Front Lines and they kept up terrible rifle fire all night. It was impossible to sleep. The Turks kept up their terrible rifle fire all night.

MAY 9

A Gurkha Mountain Battery near us fired back at the Turks all night. We did not have to fire much but during the night we had another two men killed and one wounded.

I did four hours on watch until morning. We had bully beef and biscuits for breakfast: Same for dinner. Biscuits and bacon for tea and our water bottles filled to last us 24 hours.

Most of the men on the *Lützow* knew very little about the war they had sailed into. The spotlight of international politics shone brightly on the Middle East, but it was nothing more than a dim glow in the desert training camp at Maadi. There, the focus had been on the declining state of the bloodied fields of France, the combat zone that the 5th Light Horse had originally been in training for.

"We didn't expect what we got at Anzac Cove. It was a bit of a surprise to find the Turks parked at our front door. It wasn't until later that we were able to piece together what had happened to the Tommy ships in the Dardanelles. When we got

that news, it was another surprise, and it gave us something bigger to think about."

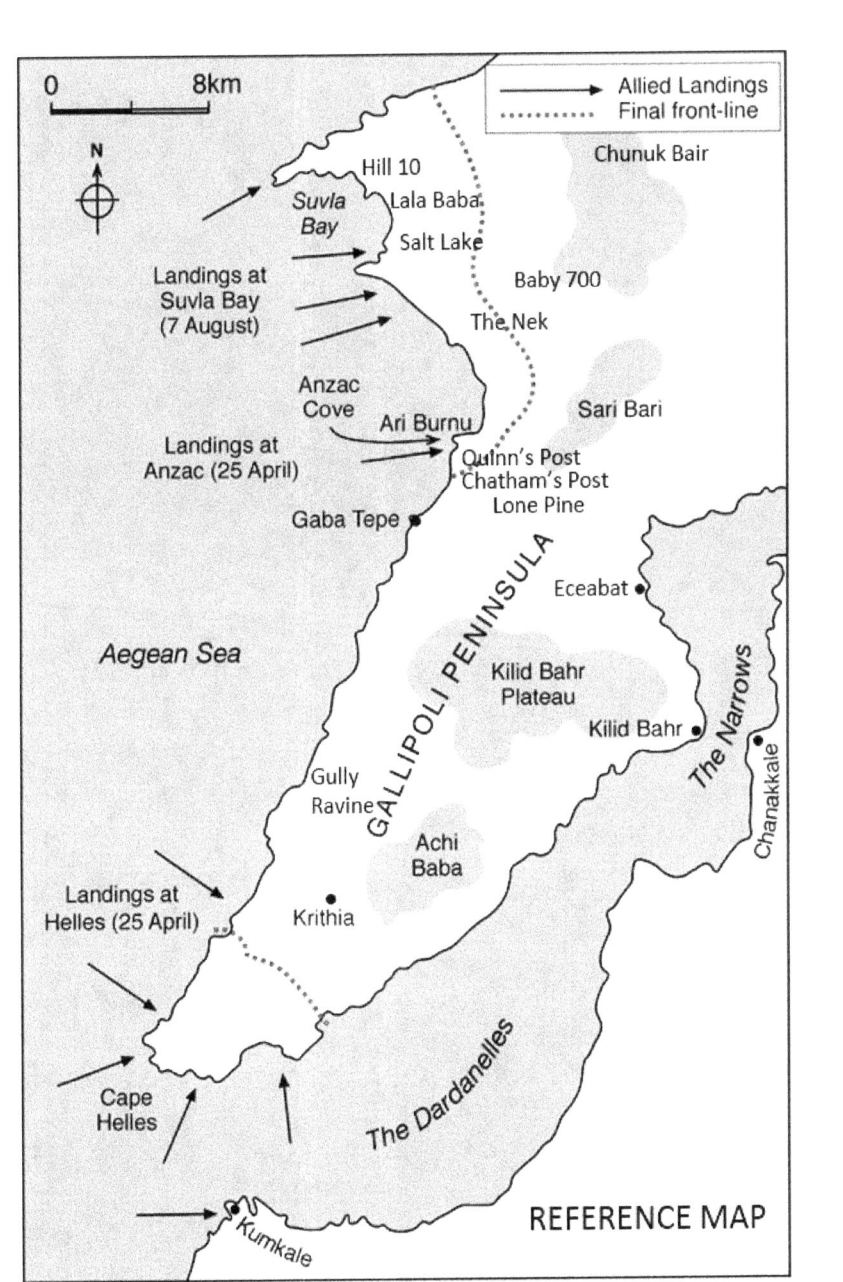

HOW THE WAR STARTED: NOT THE OFFICIAL VERSION

THE MEN OF THE 5TH Light Horse didn't know much about the beginning of the war they were thrust into. It had never been a hot topic in Egypt in the early weeks of 1915. The men of the 5th landed at Anzac Cove in a quandary. Dad's version of how the Dardanelles Campaign started came via a story written by one of the French war correspondents located at the Cove. It's what Dad told me had happened when I came home from school after being taught the version in the history books. Here's what Dad told me:

Russia, one of Britain's allies, was on the verge of civil conflict, in a dire financial state, troubled by the political unrest that threatened the Tzarist regime. The British leaders were aware of these problems, but they reasoned that their alliance with Russia would inhibit a sneaky German attack on Great Britain from the east—across the Baltic Sea past Denmark and the North Sea.

The outbreak of the war in France threatened Russia's Atlantic trade lanes through the English Channel, and an alternative sea lane was envisaged to side-step the problem: It was to run east across the Mediterranean from Gibraltar to the Aegean Sea, through the Straits of the Dardanelles to the Sea of Marmara, then through the narrow ribbon of the Bosphorus into the Black Sea to Odesa at Russia's back door.

Turkey's entry into the war on Germany's side caused sleepless nights for Britain's newly appointed Minister of Munitions, David Lloyd George, a gutsy mover with a fertile mind. No pansy, he was soon to become the powerful British Prime Minister. Lloyd George knew Turkey would oppose the Mediterranean Sea lane, and that the Turks would be likely to attack Russia from the Black Sea. If so, he reasoned that such an attack would end in a Russian defeat. If the Ottomans had Russia in the bag, and Germany conquered Denmark, Poland, Holland and the Baltic States, Great Britain could indeed be in danger of the envisioned German-Ottoman attack from the North Sea with occupied Russia as the base.

To avoid that threat, Lloyd George acted. His Empire was already locked in a terrifying conflict with Germany on the fields of France, but he knew had to move on the Middle East. The success of the alternative sea lane to Russia depended on two things—open traffic through the Dardanelles, and Russian control of the glittering Turkish seaport of Constantinople, which straddled the all-important Bosphorus, the only entry to the Black Sea.

The Ottomans knew Constantinople was in danger, but geography was on their side. Sitting a scant sixty miles to the south-west of the great city were the narrow straits of the Dardanelles, the gateway to the Sea of Mamara and the Bosphorus. These straits were bordered by Ottoman soil, on the east by the Gallipoli Peninsula and on the west by the Turkish mainland.

When whispers reached the Turkish masterminds that Winston Churchill, Lloyd George's First Lord of the Admiralty, had been urging for a sea offensive up the Dardanelles and across the Sea of Marmara to take Constantinople, they closed the Dardanelles to British ships in December 1914. They fortified the seaboards of the Gallipoli Peninsula and the shores of mainland Turkey with massive long-range gun batteries.

The straits of the Dardanelles have a wide entry from the Aegean Sea, due west of Cape Helles on the southern tip of the Gallipoli Peninsula. As the waters flow north-west, their passage shrinks to bring the Gallipoli Peninsula and the Turkish mainland closer together in what is referred to as the Dardanelles Narrows.

Guarding these treacherous narrow waters on the Turkish side was the well-armed fortress of Çanakkale. Taking no further chances, the Turks also anchored a network of mines across the Narrows, stringing them in lines at close intervals from shore to shore. There they bobbed just below the surface, their prongs sticking out like giant needles. What chance did Churchill's sea offensive have? Did anyone bother to point out that if the on-shore guns didn't get his attacking ships, the mines would? Not a whit deterred, the determined Sea Lord, in cahoots with two more of Lloyd George's upper-level naval cronies, Vice Admiral John de Robeck and Vice Admiral Sackville Carden, hit the "Go" button.

Churchill positioned his fleet of sixteen British and French battleships and cruisers off Cape Helles at the south-eastern tip of the Gallipoli Peninsula in readiness to steam straight up the thirty-eight-mile waterway of the Dardanelles, then across the Sea of Mamara to put Constantinople in his Empire trophy bag.

Alarm bells rang loudly in London where Churchill's sternest critics, aware of the counter-offensive moves of the Turks in the Dardanelles, were aghast at the boldness of his plan. Blissfully ignoring the negative carping, Lloyd George urged his buddy on. Churchill, barking orders from the bridge of his illustrious battleship, *HMS Queen Elizabeth*, aimed his armada at the Dardanelles Narrows, and steamed ahead with all flags flying to prove that Britannia ruled the waves! It was his silliest mistake. His ships sailed straight into the guns of Çanakkale and the mines of the Narrows, and his great fleet advanced no more than a few miles into the dangerous waterway.

At least six of his biggest ships, including *Irresistible, Ocean*, and the French battleship, *Bouvet*, were sunk or severely damaged. Stung by failure, and the ire of his London critics, Churchill reluctantly aborted his mission, thereby saving his other ships and what was left of his reputation.

With the sea offensive in tatters and the Dardanelles closed, the obvious alternative for Lloyd George and his London cronies was to green-light an already-planned infantry attack on the troublesome Ottoman forts on the western seaboard of Gallipoli.

What else?

The plan looked feasible: Land an army on the southern and eastern seaboards of the Peninsula; approach Gallipoli's vulnerable forts across land from the east; take them over, train their captured guns on the mines in the Narrows and the gun batteries on the Turkish mainland, and clear the Dardanelles for Churchill's second try for Constantinople.

The wheels were put in motion. Two months later, the British Commander of the Allied Army, General Sir Ian Hamilton, in company with a re-energised Churchill on *HMS Queen Elizabeth*, safely anchored off the Greek Island of Lemnos, were intent on going ahead with The Dardanelles Committee's plans for a spectacular infantry attack on the Turkish forts. The scheme had all the elements of a daring military chess game: Great Britain and her Allies versus the Ottoman Empire; a manoeuvre to be played out in bullets and blood on Turkish soil. This brazen offensive had impressive back-up. Churchill re-positioned his mighty fleet in the Aegean Sea to provide cover for Hamilton's landings on the eastern and southern beaches of the Gallipoli Peninsula. The chosen day for the Hamilton landings was Sunday, April 25, 1915. The plan fired up: The British 29th Division, a mighty task force of Allied troops, was directed to come ashore at Cape Helles, the Gallipoli Peninsula's southern tip, while another army of British regiments plus a large assignment of Australians and New Zealanders were to land at Gaba Tepe further up the eastern seaboard of the Peninsula.

These were the bishops, knights, and pawns of Hamilton's daunting offensive; a double-pronged attack. In the ANZAC quarter, thousands of fighting men were waiting aboard Churchill's battleships and destroyers to be loaded into a massive fleet of landing boats in the early morning of the approaching day. Their brief—to establish an armed stronghold on the eastern shores of Gallipoli, and to proceed from there across the hills, crags, and valleys of the hostile terrain to the back door of the massive Turkish gun batteries that guarded the Dardanelles; no more than five miles away.

After landing at Cape Helles on the same day, the Brits and their Allies had been ordered to advance on the hilly inland outpost of Achi Baba, a few miles north of the Cape. They were to make it theirs, then sweep further north to join an ANZAC advance from Gaba Tepe, for a combined attack on the Turkish forts. *All in one day!*

So sat the game plan on Sir Ian Hamilton's chessboard, a breathtaking strategy, and a pre-ordained winner! Backed by the might of the Dardanelles fleet belching fire and brimstone from their batteries of guns, a magnificent wave of gallant regiments were to be sent charging in triumph across the Gallipoli Peninsula, well on their way to the first step of a renewed plan to snatch Constantinople from the hands of the Ottomans; and all to save the troubled Russian Empire. But as history ungraciously reveals, Ian Hamilton had been playing the wrong game on the wrong chessboard, and Fate wasn't having any of it.

There was one big spanner in the works. It was later revealed that Ian Hamilton had been informed that the Turkish army was little more than a hotbed of untrained thugs and layabouts who didn't know a rifle from a liquorice stick, and he fell for it.

On the morning of April 25, 1915, the Grim Reaper, with a grin on his face, was waiting for the grand banquet to be tabled. Hamilton and Churchill, filled with optimism, were suddenly in the hot seat. What followed on that late spring morning in April was one of the biggest strategic disasters of the Twentieth Century, a major slap in the face for Great Britain, the Empire, and its Allies; a happening that was to be spoken about in hushed tones and discussed in awe for decades. In the opinions of wiser men, the Dardanelles Campaign should have been written off and forgotten that day.

Thoughtful people can never understand why it didn't happen.

CHURCHILL'S FOLLY
French Battleship Bouvet taken out by on-shore guns in the Dardanelles Narrows in 1915

Winston Churchill

ANZAC:
THE BIRTH OF THE LEGEND

AFTER THE WAR, CONFLICTING STORIES of the so-called "muddle" of the original ANZAC landing at Gallipoli on April 25, 1915, began to circulate in profusion. Fed by all kinds of rumours and stabs at the truth, the guessing games kept growing: The further Gallipoli drifted into the mists and myths of the past, the more fanciful and florid the stories became. When Dad and his mates landed at the Cove on May 8, the April 25 landing was a hot subject. Just about every surviving man from every boat had a different tale to tell—each from an individual viewpoint. Put together, these viewpoints have resulted in one confusing story, retold here to keep Dad's diary in focus,

The April ANZAC 25 landing was timed to begin after the moon went down at 3:30 a.m. Forty-eight landing boats loaded with Aussie and Kiwi infantry, under the cover of darkness, were launched from Churchill's ships and towed by power craft toward the Peninsula. Nearing the target, surprise upsets occurred. The boats were too crowded; men were anxious; they could hear the water lapping the shore, they could see the dim shapes of the high cliffs looming above them, but as the moon had gone down, they were pretty much in the dark.

When it was time to cut the tow lines to get the oars n the water to row to the beach, there were arguments about where the beach was. As the stealthy armada floundered, tow lines tangled, boats collided, and men fell over each other, some into deep water where they were forced to ditch their heavy equipment to avoid drowning. Shouted commands fell on deaf ears, and things went haywire.

When the first wave of men hit the pebble beach, there was more confusion: Vision was still limited, and no one could see exactly what was going on, but they moved as fast as they could to the rocky base of the cliffs. The second wave came ashore in the first light of dawn that exposed them to Turkish snipers and machine gunners. Braving it out, they clawed their way to the top of the cliffs to face the inland terrain of hills, ravines, ridges, and rocky outcrops. Setting foot on the beach was one thing, securing a position on the cliff tops in the first light of dawn with snipers at the ready was something else. Against the odds, they were able to return the enemy fire and hold their hard-won advantage. Into the dirt of the unwelcome hills and crags went picks and shovels that fashioned hasty dugouts in the hills close to the beach, and deeper trenches further up the rise—a mighty effort.

The result resembled a ragged picnic site, but it was more like a toehold—not all that much bigger than Sydney's Circular Quay and its approaches. In it, a tattered army of men prepared to walk, stagger or stumble into the bloodied pages of history. The Cove was theirs. There they functioned; wept, prayed, lived, or died, depending on the whims of Fate and the wisdom of the Georgie Boys in faraway London. The Peninsula playground of Anzac Cove was open for business; *and it wasn't Luna Park!*

One of the 11th Battalion men who landed on April 25 disputed the familiar story about a *"wrong beach."* He told Dad that there was only ever one beach, and it was the one at Anzac Cove, the curved strip just north of Gaba Tepe. The *"wrong beach"* landing is mentioned in official documents as one of the mistakes that caused the failure of the landing. Dad's friend was adamant that when the 11th landed in the light of dawn, they realised that although the cliffs above them were uneven and rough, the beach they'd landed on had better cover from the Turkish guns at Gaba Tepe, and that's where the ANZAC garrison was set up—on the *right beach*! Dad didn't argue or ask questions, he took his friend's word.

History indicates that luck was not smiling on the ANZACs on the disastrous Sunday morning of April 25. That's a simple enough appraisal of what is still regarded as a *bloody mess,* because, simply put, the alleged rabble of the Turkish army turned the tables on the invaders.

Here's how they did it:

On the crucial eve of Saturday, April 24, while Hamilton was waiting patiently for his offensive to launch, Turkish spies on the Greek islands were reporting large numbers of Allied soldiers boarding troop ships in the Aegean Sea. Later in the same evening, lookouts on Gallipoli spied Churchill's battleships cruising in formation in the soft light of the waning moon just north of the Greek island of Imbros.

Ottoman masterminds had expected an enemy invasion somewhere along Gallipoli's mid-eastern seaboard, but they were unable to pinpoint the exact location. Rightly guessing that the invasion was finally happening, the Turks uncoiled their battle springs, greased their rifles, assembled their machine guns, had a word with Allah, and sprang into immediate action. Word flashed like lightning up and down the lines of Turkish soldiers positioned on the scrubby hills for miles to the north and south of Gaba Tepe. They proved to be smarter than Ian Hamilton was told, but perhaps not as lucky as they could have been.

Dad was of this opinion:

> *"If the Turks had sent all their soldiers to Gaba Tepe instead of stringing them out for miles north and south, the Allied regiments would have all been cut down as soon as they set foot on the beaches. The Turks converged on Gaba Tepe later in the morning, but they came too late."*

THE INFAMOUS LANDING: GLORIFIED TRUTH IN PRINT

THE INFAMOUS ANZAC LANDING of 1915 was born to be a critical target.

As an important part of the first Allied assault on the Gallipoli Peninsula, it was the linchpin of the eastern seaboard offensive and it was launched with great hope for success. While it wasn't a complete disaster, it didn't fulfil its part of the overall plan. The ANZACs landed. They took possession of the beach, established their stronghold in accordance with their orders, did it in record time, but failed to push the Turks out of the way to kickstart their ordered advance across the Peninsula to attack the Dardanelles gun batteries.

They got no further than the cliffs at Anzac Cove; there they were trapped, and that was never supposed to happen.

Once more, alarm bells rang in London. Excuses, apologies, and accusations rumbled around the military boardrooms, and desperate minds searched for ways to right the wrong!

While the official rush to get Hamilton's ill-fated offensive back on track went ahead, the war correspondents, ordered by the top brass to pull something positive out of the failure bag, shifted their attention to the ANZAC landing and lit up the human element: They wrote vividly about men in all kinds of trouble in the boats; leaping first into the water then charging in dutiful haste for the beach, and to hell with obstacles and the hostile terrain.

Charging on through the *rat-a-tat-tat* of machine guns and the relentless *snap-crackle-and-pop* of rifle fire, red hot bullets *pinging* against rocks, spent shells dancing in the air, men fell and stumbled to be picked up by those who followed.

Heroic efforts of soldiers dragging their wounded mates to the safety of overhanging rocks were lauded in reports filed by correspondents who whipped up an outpouring of gallant words. One on them embellished his story with references to the dogged courage and back-slapping bravery of men who urged each other on with *the kind of yelps and good-natured yelling you'd hear at a regatta on the Thames.*

It was rousing stuff; the kind that seasoned newsmen lived for. It caught the eye and held it; headlines and words designed to have the newsboys of London yelling themselves hoarse in Piccadilly Circus and Trafalgar Square.

There have been people who twigged that such effusive reports from Gallipoli had been fancied-up to keep the home fires burning brightly, and to counter continuing bad news from the French Front. *That's never been proven.*

Back home in Australia, news editors, hungry for information, tended to leap on colourful stories and rousing copy. Even as long ago as 1915 a fanciful editor never allowed facts to get in the way of a grabby headline or gutsy words. Fleet Street was in marvellous shape back then; it was an honoured London address in the print world of Australia, where its diatribes were almost as hallowed as chapters in the Bible.

But as time went by, it has not been all hearts and flowers for the Down Under boys. Among the many positive words written and published about the ANZACs on Gallipoli, are piqued references to the frequent omissions of fighting men from other Allied countries; in particular—Great Britain, Canada, France, and India. In some cases, these omissions have added lustre to the ANZAC name. Even today, the greatest glories of Gallipoli still seem to belong to Australia and New Zealand. Such is the power of media accounts that morph into tributes upon relentless repetition.

The fact is that nobody was shopping for accolades or garlands on Gallipoli. They were too busy trying to understand what was happening while they did their best to stay in one piece. Under such circumstances it's easy to see how the ANZAC landing came alive on a litany of real or imagined *"what-ifs"*:

What if the boat lines hadn't tangled; *what if* there hadn't been a mistake about the beach; *what if* the boats hadn't collided; *what if* the men hadn't been thrown into the water; *what if* it hadn't been so dark; *what if* the Turks hadn't been prepared. It's the *"what-ifs"* that prompt the most challenging question:

What would have happened if they hadn't happened? Similarly with the *Titanic: What if the iceberg hadn't been there?*

To sharpen the point in this case, Australia and New Zealand were the youngest colonies in the war, yet their virgin soldiers acquitted themselves like veterans despite the massive wall of setbacks. It made for richly melodramatic reading; an example of which occurred in the printed quotes of Sir William Birdwood, the General in charge of the ANZAC landing when he addressed his men on the shore:

> *"You have got through the difficult business (the landing) now you have only to dig, dig, dig, until you are safe."*

Dig-dig-dig: the inspiration for the mining ditty from Disney's *Snow White and the Seven Dwarfs*? And this next directive made at midnight:

> *"You must organise entrenchments and hold on with all your might. Please complete the entrenching scheme. and link up firing line trenches with those on right and left.*

And there you have it: Virgin soldiers steadfastly rising to the job as ordered by their gold-braided heavy, Sir William Birdwood, soon to be known on Gallipoli as "The Boss." In other reports of the ANZAC landing, the *dig-dig-dig* speech is accredited to Sir Ian Hamilton, an altogether better choice. After pulling the 5th Light Horsemen out of Egypt to fight in the trenches as infantry, *without their Walers,* he owed them something; even it was little more than a few kind words and one pretty-please:

> Rudyard Kipling: *You're a better man than I am, Gunga Din*

In the end, the ongoing belief that the ANZAC morning was etched in tragedy and untimely error, only serves to highlight the Shakespearean aura that unceasingly envelopes it: History implies it should never have happened as it did, and that's the final clue to its fascination. Fate's hand moved against the young soldiers from Australia and New Zealand and made them immortal.

So was born, in human minds, the undeniable spirit of the men we have come to celebrate; overpraised in contemporary print of the time perhaps, but in real life, one of the most amazing examples of the do-or-die spirit ever seen on a battlefield.

And for that very reason, in the early seventies, sixty years after the sun rose on that fateful morning, Australia's Anzac Day made a blockbuster comeback that rekindled its lost lustre. It was brought out of the shadows and given back to everyday people who had forgotten for a while how important it had been. Like the prodigal son, Anzac Day, kept alive by the undying mystique that created it in the first place, came back to the fold all by itself. With the ranks of Gallipoli survivors in rapid decline, a reborn interest swept into the younger generations and continued into the new millennium.

Annual visits to Gallipoli on Anzac Day have since become "the thing" for young people, and not because of any fleeting trend. Dad didn't live to see that and I'm so sad he didn't.

THE RIVER CLYDE

The British Trojan Horse caught in a hail of bullets at Cape Helles on April 25

CAPE HELLES:
IAN HAMILTON STRIKES AGAIN

ANZAC COVE DID NOT HAVE sole rights to the Hamilton drama of April 25. What went on, *or off*, at the Cove was matched by five landings at Cape Helles on that same day. The might of the Allies included the famous Lancashire Fusiliers, who emerged as heroes.

These landings are worth a look because they were to have an enormous effect on the future of the ANZACs:

Cape Helles, on the southern tip of the pear-shaped Gallipoli Peninsula, hardly more than five miles wide, was chosen for the five Allied landings that wrapped around it like a glove. First prize went to an ingenious trick to out-fox the Turks—the Brit's answer to the Trojan Horse.

BERTHED IN THE NEARBY WATERS of the Greek island of Lemnos, sat the *River Clyde*, a decommissioned four-thousand-ton coal boat, sent to the Middle East by the Royal Navy to be used as a landing craft. On the eve of the Cape Helles attack, its cavernous storage space was filled with more than two-thousand troops. Come the dawn, it was powered up and sent charging at full speed to the curved western beach of the Cape, where it rammed into an outcrop eighty yards from the shore.

While the Turks appeared to ignore it, its cargo of soldiers raced out to join the fray. The foxy Turks waited, then opened fire. It was a massacre that few survived by ducking back into the boat. In a day of disasters, casualties and death on both sides, the *River Clyde* misfire stood tall.

Still, the gallant nine-year-old ship turned out to be a real pain in the butt for the Turks, who did their best to knock it out. It stayed tightly wedged where it was until the long-delayed December evacuation. During the campaign, its condensers were used to make fresh water, it was a shady Dressing Station for the wounded, a safe holding place for reserve troops and for men who needed to take their boots off and have a smoke. After the war, *River Clyde* was fixed up, sold to the Spaniards, and continued to ply the Mediterranean as a tramp steamer until 1965.

In 1919, a few heavies in London wanted her to be taken home to be anchored on the docks to be shown off as a sentimental symbol of the Gallipoli war, but outraged cries of *"You've got to be kidding!"* scotched that idea.

When Dad landed in May, *River Clyde* was part of the Cape Helles landscape, clearly visible from the Cove, and one of the war's permanent attractions.

Dad told me that the men at the Cove liked seeing her there because it meant that the Tommies were still around.

NOBODY WAS THROWING CONFETTI AND streamers at the Allied grab for Cape Helles on the morning of April 25. The Turk's nastiest trick was to lace the shallow approaches to the beaches with rolls of barbed wire that tore at the men who failed to see them. As they struggled to free themselves, they were caught in the fire from Turkish trench lines due north of the Cape.

Against such brutal odds, the Allies still managed to set themselves up as a fortified encampment on Cape Helles, but the planned advance on Achi Baba had been nipped in the bud, and the attack was on the back foot. The gloriously touted Gallipoli invasion that was meant to be Hamilton's Everest, had missed its place in the sun. Counting the landings at Anzac Cove, the score for that morning was not in Hamilton's favour. When that depressing news filtered into the polished boardroom of the elite Dardanelles Committee, the gilt-framed pictures on the wall would have been looking down on limply held cigars dangling from the lips of the Georgie Boys as they mumbled their vexing question: *"How do we fix the unfixable?"*

THE ANZAC CAMPSITE: NOT THE COVE HILTON

AT ANZAC COVE, THE HANGOUT for Dad and his 5th Light Horse mates, the trenches of the Australian Front Line faced the Turks in their trenches, barely a decent spit away on the ridges of the uneven high ground above the beach. Behind the Front Line were the Cove's support trenches; a second line of defense in case of attack. Behind them again were the reserve trenches to provide back-up if needed. Further down were the dugouts cut into the rocky walls in the unwelcome face of the cliffs; dodgy resting places for men not on duty, but able to supply elements of safety from the continued Turkish bombardments.

The Cove was no Aegean Shangri-La. Its trenches became muddy, dirty, and lice ridden. They were no more than deep holes in the ground dug in zig-zag lines as shelter from bullets and bombs, and protected by sandbags lined along the top, and functioning as turrets. Hygiene was a blurred word at the Cove; at best, necessary; at worst, primitive, and in pristine company better not spoken about. Dad did anyway. He described them as:

> *"Little better than a falling-down backyard dunny in Rocky, and that it was no good being shy; it was one-pit-one-seat-for-all and you were a stuffed shirt if you didn't see the funny side."*

Further down the rise from the trenches, and closer to the beach, were the crude shelters for the commanding officers and a dressing station for the wounded, where the most critical awaited transfer to the hospital ships in the Aegean Sea; and then, in extreme cases, to base hospitals on Malta or on the Greek islands.

The Cove's rickety pontoon jetty serviced supply boats coming in from Egypt and the Greek islands bearing food, water, and ammunition: Despite its lacklustre appointments, Anzac Cove was non-stop peak-hour action, an encampment that had none of the comforts of home, and few of the trappings of civilisation. Yet, according to scores of reports from various sources, a certain amount of levity managed to keep the men's spirits from evaporating completely—cricket games, concerts, and other diversions. Dad didn't talk much about stuff like that, he stayed focused on his diary.

He was never interested in parties and party talk. In his vintage years, he joined a bowls club and had a stab at perfecting the art of rolling bowling balls, but he never hung around the bar "gasbagging."

Like everyone else at the Cove, he was into the beach, even though it was constantly under Turkish sniper fire. But as the battle raged with no end in sight, battle-weary men; bloodied, muddied and riddled with lice, often braved the eagle-eyed enemy snipers for the sheer heaven of moments in the cool blue water, so bright and clean that pebbles on the seafloor were visible.

HERE FOLLOWS THE OVERVIEW OF Gallipoli in the late spring of 1915:

The men of the 5th in the front-line trenches were not alone; they had robust mates on left and right: The New Zealand Infantry, the Australian 11th Battalion, the 1st Australian Infantry Brigade and a mountain battery held by the British Gurkhas who had landed north of the Cove on April 25.

Twelve Miles further away on the southern point of the Peninsula, the Allied British and French regiments were locked down on the beaches of Cape Helles.

Turkish regiments on the high ground of the impregnable Achi Baba and its neighbouring ridges and ravines kept their eagle eyes on the Cape and the Cove. They had the best of it; close contact with the western Dardanelles fortress of Çanakkale and other towns, villages and supply posts on the Turkish mainland, where tens of thousands of Ottoman reinforcements waited for the call to battle. For Dad's mates in the Cove, it seemed anything but an even fight. Ironically, the azure blue Aegean Sea, the Dardanelles, the Gallipoli Peninsula, and the eastern mainland of Turkey are among the most beautiful geographical landmarks of the north-eastern Mediterranean. In the literary world, they were the long-ago haunts of the mythical gods of Olympus, elevated to legend by the tales of the Iliad, the sirens of Ulysses, the glory of ancient Troy, and the matchless paradise of the Greek Islands.

One observer has likened them to *Peter Pan's Neverland*, and in the early decades of the Twentieth Century, they were among the most desirable play places for the wanton and wealthy of the New World. Their unavailability for hedonistic purposes in the summer of 1915, two years before America entered the war, put the noses of the travelling nouveau riche out of kilter. Worse still, nobody could tell them how long they'd have to wait for their azure paradises to return to normal.

At Anzac Cove, plonked fairly in the middle of these azure paradises, the question everyone asked was: *How long will this be going on?*

MAY 10

It rained in the Front Line last night, just enough to make things very wet and miserable. Went back to reserve trenches this morning. The Turks kept up very heavy rifle fire all night and they were sending up star shells as well. We had three men wounded. I was down on the beach for about an hour and a half and came back carrying ammunition; it was a hard pull lugging it up the hill.

Later I went to help dig a big wide path below the Front Line to take the wounded men down to the Dressing Station. Seven or eight stretcher-bearers were getting sniped every day.

MAY 11

Went up to the Front Line again this morning:

The Turks attacked the New Zealanders on our left last night. We were in reserve while the attack was on, but the Turks were driven off before they attacked us. This morning we could see the Tommies at Cape Helles shelling Achi Baba, a few miles to their north-east and a fair way south-east of us, but we had a quiet day apart from a fair amount of shell fire.

THE TANGLED WEB
OF THE MIDDLE EAST

ACHI BABA TURNED OUT TO be the Bad Guy, the key to the Allies downfall.

As the original target of the failed Cape Helles landings, it was a high well-fortified hill, with a dress-circle view of both the Peninsula and Dardanelles narrows. Clearly visible to the east were Anzac Cove, the neighbouring Gully Ravine on the peninsula's seaboard, and to the south-southeast, the Allied regiments at Cape Helles. Achi Baba was the Turk's secret weapon, the ultimate strategic kingpin, and they were determined to hold it no matter what.

By now, Dad and his mates were in daily contact with the Peninsula Grapevine, a gossipy news service passing from mouth to ear, and trench to trench, a soldier hotline that picked up on what was happening everywhere and kept everyone up to date. Dad and his mates depended on it because it had a reliable track record. They knew precious little about the convoluted politics of the Middle East and even less about the whys of the war on Gallipoli.

For the 5th Light Horsemen, Gallipoli had come out of the blue. They were equally uninformed about the Dardanelles, Constantinople, The Sea of Marmara and The Bosphorus but they were learning fast. The more they learned, the more their awareness of what they were doing on Gallipoli grew. They soon realised they were cogs in the wheels of a conflict that was even bigger and more fearful than they had first imagined.

Dad said it was no use getting all hot and bothered with everything, so the lads just got on with the job and hoped for the best.

A NEW DETERMINATION GREW AS the Grapevine delivered more information. It was obvious that the war was not going to be over as soon as everyone wanted. Day by day, men were living to survive another day, and another day was often another day to survive, often a day when hopes and prayers were dashed. For some, it would be a day to die. The one thing that didn't die was the determination to bring it all to the right end. The wised-up enemy, at home on the familiar terrain of the rugged Peninsula, were anything but willing to invite the ANZACs to a seaside barbecue.

Many of my father's mates, men and boys from Barcaldine and Blackall he'd trained with in Australia and Egypt, failed to make the trenches; gone on the first day. The men of the 5th had charged into hell with their eyes closed to the facts, no fault of their own. Gone were the vigorous days of training in the Egyptian desert—the message was shattering and crystal clear: it was going to be a savage war, and the Turkish masterminds were in no mood to be throwing salutes at the Union Jack or the Southern Cross.

They had decisive runs on the board: They paid out on Churchill's overblown plans for his mighty fleet in the Dardanelles, and there was no way they were going to let the Allies run all over Constantinople, idolised by the Ottomans as the Queen City of the Middle East. There she sat in all her Muslim glory, owning the Harbour of the Golden Horn, and straddling the Bosphorus, the naturally beautiful waterway that linked the Sea of Marmara to the Black Sea and Russia. If Churchill's navy could find a new way to get their hands on Constantinople, Turkish dominance in the Middle East would be no more.

The great city was steeped in exotic history that stretched back in time to the Roman and Byzantium Empires. Her international glamour was enhanced by her position as the starting point of the original *Orient Express*, which ran directly to Paris via Budapest and Vienna. It was well patronised by European royalty and the world's upper crust travellers, who came to throw their millions at the great seaport's aesthetic attractions while they waited to board the luxury train. The big boys in London were having themselves on if they thought Constantinople could be ripped away without a mighty fight.

In the early months of 1915, Tzarist Russia, plagued by swiftly escalating disenchantment with Nicolas II, had frantically grabbed at the promised Mediterranean Sea lane as the solution to its problems. Greedy Russian eyes locked on Constantinople; they wanted her all right; beyond that they needed her, and the Allies were prepared to spill blood to take her. It was becoming more obvious to keen observers that the underlying element of the Dardanelles Campaign was a desperate push by Lloyd George to keep Russia solvent by a successful takeover of Constantinople and its rich treasures.

There was another reason. It was known in political circles that Lloyd George wanted the Ottoman Empire taken out. In his opinion, there was only room for one Empire in the Twentieth Century, and the Ottoman model wasn't it! Apart from Lloyd George's motives, troubled Russia's link to the war ran deeper. The Ottomans and Russians despised each other with a passion fuelled by ancestral blood. Sixty years earlier, in the mid-1800s, the Russian army had smashed the Ottomans in the Crimean War, and the Turks had no desire to see the rich cultural treasures of their Queen City dirtied by the grime of the grubby Russian peasants.

If that wasn't enough to keep the pot bubbling, there was yet another spider weaving a web: Among those said to have looked with disfavour on the 1915 move to give military support to the Russian sea lane, was none other than Britain's King George V. Two years into the future, in 1917, the British Monarch would refuse help to his first cousin Tzar Nicolas II after the fall of the Russian Empire. This refusal was to be seen by many as a heartless move by King George to distance himself from his German bloodline, a sensitive issue for many of his subjects at the time. Nicolas shared George's bloodline. In 1918, the Tzar and his family, by then prisoners of the Bolshevik revolutionaries, would be murdered in captivity.

It has since been alleged that George V could have saved them by offering asylum in London, an offer the Bolsheviks would have honoured; if not, they may have risked displeasure with Britain; a situation they could not afford. But if George were to rescue Nicolas and his family, London would then have been home to two royal families with German bloodlines. With Germany geared to make a grab for England, how long would it have been before the British population reacted negatively to the expensive presence in London of two royal German bloodlines? No wonder the Middle East was a stewpot, a pot that included regiments of gallant men from Australia and New Zealand; men who were fast becoming aware of why the pot was bubbling and why they were in it.

A short five months earlier the 5th Light Horseman had spent Christmas at sea, well on their way to the sunny desert sands of Egypt. How much did any of them know about David Lloyd George? Were any of them aware of the political intrigues that involved Imperial Russia in a dangerous scheme to snatch Constantinople from the Turks? Would they have known about George V's possible uneasiness about sharing a German bloodline with an outlawed Russian Tzar? It was the second week of May, and the picture was becoming clearer: During all this political intrigue, strategic wrangling, bubbling stew pots and outright bloody warring, the ever-changing drama of the Allied offensive in the Middle East proceeded to sail grandly on, seriously hampered by something that looked very much like a busted rudder.

MAY 12

The Turks shelled our trenches again last night.

I was on the ground up front on outpost. For the first time, I had to lie flat as machine-gun fire was very hot. I got back into the trenches just before daylight. The 1st Infantry Brigade on our right lost a lot of men. We had two wounded.

MAY 13

Rained just a little last night: We are still in the Firing Line:

Nothing much happened last night but today the Turkish snipers were very busy. We had over 20 men killed or wounded going down to the beach.

I joined the call for volunteers to lay barbed wire in front of our trenches.

A man was shot dead beside me and two more were wounded. I brought them to safety, but one died on the way down to the Dressing Station near the beach.

May 13 was a Thursday, not yet a week since the landing of my father's regiment. Things were far from flash. Nothing much had changed; terrible food, sleepless nights, the lurking danger of enemy snipers, the uncertainty of seeing another sunrise, the distress of wounded men not yet evacuated to the hospital ships; nights alive with rifle fire, star shells and death.

Dad's vocabulary is limited: "awful" seems like an understatement, but he resorts to its use a lot and it does hit the target. He does not write anywhere yet of his personal feelings; he goes into no detail about the wounded men, but we assume the worst. There's detachment in these early accounts, bland acceptance of a situation he's doing his best to come to terms with. Thousands of men living day to day, driven by a resolve to have everything end in their favour: Who could blame them for feeling frustrated and hopeless? Yet, so far there's no evidence of that in my father's writing, so it is assumed that these men bore their plight with the kind of strength and courage that most of us never need to reach for. Gallipoli's message provides a many-layered view of the human condition under stress.

All the time, day after day, the anxious call running up and down the Allied lines was: "Take Achi Baba!" That was it! "Take Achi Baba, take the gun batteries, blow up the mines, let's win the war and go home!"

So why wasn't someone doing it?

Perilously close to the Australian Front Line at Anzac Cove were the Turkish trenches, the ever-present enemy breathing the same air, with sniper rifles at the ready. *Move into the open at Anzac Cove and Goodbye world!*

If you're an avid reader, you'll find as you plough through books on the history of warfare from the dim dark ages to whenever, that the names of soldiers, doctors, nurses, and any other rank-and-file people involved in any way in any war, are rarely included in any of the plans and strategies of the battles being fought. Such factors and decisions are confined to heavies like those in the David Lloyd George cartel in the London of 1914-18.

On their heads rested the successes or failures of Gallipoli. Consequently, it has been noted by scores of anti-war historians that soldiers and fighting men in the Dardanelles Campaign were there to take orders without question:

> ALFRED LORD TENNYSON: *The Charge of the Light Brigade: Ours is not to reason why; ours but to do and die.*

That's the accepted rule book of war, and Gallipoli's critics have jumped on it, negatively quoting Tennyson to back up their opinions; namely that Gallipoli was all about "The Empire" and the frantic need to keep it on its pedestal: To accomplish that, ordinary fighting men were sacrificed.

Looking at it broadly, the critics have a case: We all know about hallowed war heroes- generals, captains, colonels, and admirals—Patten, MacArthur, Churchill, Mountbatten, Montgomery, Rommel, Nelson, Halsey, Wellington, Eisenhower, and so on. Their names are golden in history, and we are inclined to forget that for every one of them there had to be millions of ordinary men backing them up. Now and again an Alvin York or an Audie Murphy or a Douglas Bader or an Alf Shout appears on lists of acclaimed heroes, and we all know someone who lost a soldier, a flyer, a sailor, a nurse, a daughter, a husband, or a son somewhere in some fight. And we all know is that such losses left empty spaces never again to be filled in millions of lives.

Dad was philosophical. He said that after a while it was better not to notice when someone took a bullet or didn't come back after a swim. There was nothing anyone could do. "We all got hardened fast."

WARS HAVE BEEN FOUGHT AND they'll always be fought. Punch-ups with spears and arrows, bullets and bazookas, nuclear weapons and atom bombs are the way of the world. It's all going on and on. Yes: Gallipoli critics have a case; so too, does Lord Tennyson.

But there's something else that is often overlooked. Deep in the hearts of men and women who fight when they decide they must, there surely exists an empowering spirit of responsibility that sows the seeds of an everlasting hope that one day, it will all end in perfect peace, the peace of ordinary men living ordinary lives, free from the kind of corruption and power-mad greed that drives fractured minds to think up reasons to make a war. My father was on Gallipoli; one man among many men, all doing a job they'd enlisted to do. How could they have known they would be fighting in a war that would one day be talked about as one of the biggest blunders in military history?

Dad had been on Gallipoli for five days that must have felt like an eternity, and at this point, he had no inkling of how much longer he'd be there.

All he knew was that he was there until it was over.

THEY HAD TO COME: THE KILLING FIELDS

MAY 14

Still in the Front Line:

Things were pretty quiet last night but today there's a lot of machine gunfire. I had a decent sleep last night, the first for some time. We all received some mail today. I got a letter from My Darling and one from Bella: The mail was sent on to us from Egypt and made us all a little more cheerful. I have not had a wash since we landed here and cannot get enough water to drink.

Not enough water! Par for the course on the Cove: *How to dehydrate in a trench.* May was the last month of spring on Gallipoli, the mild weather was getting ready to pack it in, and the notorious north-eastern Mediterranean summer was revving up. Nice of Georgie's Boys to pick the worst season of the year to keep the war-works happening . . .

> At this point, Dad opened up. *"We could feel the warm weather on the way. It would not be good for the Tommies; we Queenslanders all knew what summer was; most of them didn't, but Georgie's boys wouldn't have thought about that."*

NOTE: *My Darling* (note the capitals, as written) is my mother Kitty. *Bella* was my father's younger sister. Messages from home with its warm beds, fresh bread, clean air, and loving smiles. Letters from home turned out to be a spirit booster that came at the right time. A showdown was on the way, and it would be no one-day shootout! It was to come without warning to let the men of the First Division know for sure what war was really all about.

In the hills and ravines west of the Cove's First Division trenches, the Turks were grouping for their first major charge on the enemy. They'd had enough, and they were not playing games.

Here there is more confusion with dates. Official reports list the date of this assault as May 19; others say May 12, which is officially listed as the date of the 5th Light Horse departure from Alexandra.

Something's way out of kilter. If Dad and his 5th Light Horse mates were listed as being on the way from Egypt to Anzac Cove on May 12, how come they were already there preparing for a Turkish attack?

Dad's diary says the first Turkish attack on Anzac Cove happened on Sunday, May 16, not Wednesday, May 19. How could he have messed that date up? It was his wake-up call, his first real clash with the enemy and it would have been a day to remember.

Conflicting dates aside, it really doesn't matter when this juggernaut descended on the Cove; descend it did, and there are no doubts about the demons that rode in with it.

MAY 15

We came off the Front Line at daylight this morning and went to the reserve trenches. After two hours rest, we went to digging a gun road until four o'clock in the afternoon. It was a very hot day. We came back to the reserve trenches for bully beef and biscuits and went back to the Front Line for the night. The Turks were shelling heavily, and their machine-gun fire was hot: they sent over a message that if we did not surrender, they would drive us into the sea.

MAY 16

The Turks attacked our lines at daylight this morning in massed formation.

They are still at it: The rifle fire and machine-gun fire is awful. They have kept it up all day, but we were forced to mow them down in hundreds. The battleships at sea are shelling them but they are still attacking our positions. We have just had orders that we have to hold our line to the last man. We have lost about 25 men so far. The Turks got close to some of our trenches but were driven out by the New Zealanders.

MAY 17

The Turks are still attacking and have been all night, but we are still holding them. They have brought up a fresh division, the 11th Turkish Division, the pick of the Turkish Army. The 8th Light Horse has sent over a message for replacements, but we are hard-pressed and can't spare a man. It is a real nightmare. Men are being carried out dead. Two nights without sleep and the Turks are still coming.

MAY 18

The Turks attacked all night but stopped at daylight this morning until about eight o'clock. Then they came again but we will not let them get through.

Now we have had no sleep and hardly anything to eat since the attacks started two days ago. The battleship Triumph has been shelling them all day and they have lost heavily. There are thousands of Turkish dead in front of our trenches. It is awful to see them all heaped up, but we are still determined that they won't break our line.

MAY 19

The Turks stopped attacking last night but we have 'stood to' for hours waiting for them to reform. They have been sending up star shells all night and shelling our trenches. We have lost another nine men, and we have had no water and nothing to eat for twelve hours but we do not feel hungry. Everyone has a ghastly look because we have not had a wash for a week or more.

The first time I read these entries I had to take a breather to go again.

Dad's expression *"forced to mow them down"* came out of nowhere.

Mow them down doesn't seem like something my father would have thought or said, but there it was—penned by the gentle man I had known all my life. The fighting had turned a corner: Gallipoli was on the way to becoming the killing field history would call it. The message: Kill or be killed; them or us; the unwritten law of that war. Live or die. Stand up and hit back; or back off, give up, and take your chances with the Grim Reaper.

Dad and his First Division mates played the game they were forced to play.

So did the Turkish soldiers, who fought like demons for the glory of the Ottoman Empire.

Is this how it was with The Charge of the Light Brigade; at Waterloo and The Alamo or The Battle of Little Big Horn and other famous battles that rose to greatness in the face of certain death; the unavoidable taking of lives when the cause is righteous enough: the fateful irony of destiny's heroes? Poems have been written about the grandeur of ill-fated courage.

Whether Custer's men at Little Big Horn or the lancers of the Light Brigade were aware of how they were to be lauded in literature is unlikely.

Is there anything more courageous than the armada of small boats that dared the dangers of Dunkirk to haul trapped British garrisons off the beaches of northern France in the early days of World War Two?

In May of 1915, the ANZACs on Gallipoli were in no position to know they were making history while the battles they were fighting were turning them into killers with no option to be otherwise.

There's an unlikely taint of melodrama in some of my father's sentences relating to the attack of the Turks. Had they been spoken by Errol Flynn or Tom Hanks in a Hollywood movie they would be hailed as Hero Speak, accompanied by mood lighting and a plush soundtrack:

> *"If we do not surrender, they will drive us into the sea."*

> *"They have been attacking all night and we are still holding them."*

"We have just had orders to hold our line to the last man."

"They came again, but we will not let them get through."

"We have had no water and nothing to eat for twelve hours but we do not feel hungry."

These lines were written by an Aussie jackaroo who had never seen a stage play or motion picture with sound. Then again, although my father was no culture vulture, he had certainly read and reacted to the words of Rudyard Kipling and Banjo Patterson. He thought Sidney Carton's closing speech in the Charles Dickens French Revolution novel, *A Tale of Two Cities* was the epitome of self-sacrifice. When I was still a kid, he took me to revivals of the thirties movie version to hear actor Ronald Colman's voice-over delivery of Sidney Carton's last line on the very steps of the guillotine. The noble Carton has essayed a daring mission impossible; the release of a condemned friend from the Bastille by substituting himself, thereby taking his friend's place in death.

> RONALD COLMAN AS SIDNEY CARTON: *It is a far, far better thing that I do, than I have ever done; it is a far, far rest that I go to than I have ever known.*

The line's power lies in its motivation: Sidney's unrequited love for his friend's wife, and a long-ago promise that he would give his life for her if ever the time came. I'm happy to report that the Dad I knew was an old-school softie, and a romantic to boot. Okay, so who wrote, *"mow them down"*?

Mum said she asked him about that. He said he wrote it when he was almost mindless over the fury of the battle. She asked him if he wanted it kept in the diary. He said: "People need to know what happens to people in a war so they can think twice about starting another one".

The expression "stood to" in my father's diary means "at the ready," and "at the ready" means equipment, attitude, full dress; boots and all; and all for as long as it takes. No slacking off to feel sorry for yourself.

This was not Hollywood. The blood was not ketchup; the wounds were not fake; the bullets were not blanks, the bayonets were not plastic; the explosions were not CGI, and the director was not yelling "*Action!*" This was Gallipoli 1915, and it was as real as it gets.

MAY 20

The Turks have not renewed their attack yet, but we are still in the trenches waiting for them. Things were pretty quiet last night. We got half a bottle of water this morning, and some bacon and biscuits.

The Turkish dead in front of the trenches are beginning to smell; they say there are nearly seven thousand all along the lines and if they are left there it will be awful. The Turks have been very quiet all day; just a little rifle fire. The quietest day we have had since we landed.

MAY 21

We came out of the trenches this morning after a quiet night and went down to the beach for a rest. I did two hours on outpost in front of the trenches, but things were very quiet. The Turks have had enough of it. We went down to the sea and had a swim but while we were in the water the Turks shelled us and we lost two men killed and five wounded. We slept all day.

The shell fire was very heavy over our camp, but we had no more casualties. We stayed in our own dugouts all day.

MAY 22

I was working all night carrying up shells for the guns. Things are still quiet in the Front Line. We moved around to the Lone Pine to relieve the 11th Battalion at 5:30 p.m. but we are not going back into our Front-Line trenches until tomorrow. The stink of rotting bodies is something awful and we are wearing our gas masks. The Front Line smells terrible and we have to sleep the night in the reserves.

Dad and his mates taking advantage of a quiet day to hit the beach for a swim. Here's the first mention of the infamous Lone Pine, named for the one remaining pine tree in a forest of pines felled by the Turks, then cut into logs to fortify and cover the heavy line of trenches they dug on the site. Lone Pine sat about two miles over rough terrain to the south-west of the Cove.

Due west of Lone Pine, a scant four miles away, were the narrows of the Dardanelles, and the elusive seaboard guns; so near yet so far; and so damned frustrating. The location's closeness to the western seaboard gun batteries gave it strategic importance. If Achi Baba fell to the Allies, facilitating an advance up the Peninsula, ANZAC control of Lone Pine would be vital to the success of the offensive.

The 11th Battalion's recent attack had been successful, but the enemy had re-captured it a week or so later and added to the fortifications. The fight for possession of Lone Pine was an exchange of forces that continued through June and July and came to a head in a bloody battle in August.

MAY 23

We had a good sleep last night in reserve.

Went into the Front-Line trenches early this morning: The stench is almost unbearable. The Turkish dead are lying close to us. At 10 o'clock the Turks ran up white flags all along their lines, but we suspected a trick and shot the flags down. They kept putting them up all day. One of our Generals went out under a flag of truce to investigate. There was no trick. The Turks want an armistice to bury their dead. A German General was brought into our lines under a flag of truce. The enemy has been granted nine hours to get the burial detail done and we'll all be glad when it's over.

More mess-ups with dates here: Most accounts list the date of the truce as May 21. It's Dad's diary against official documentation. If he's wrong, he's two days late but what are forty-eight hours in an account like this? I can't contest the date issue. The most crucial factor is this: He was there, he was involved, he recorded what happened and I can't contest that either.

MAY 24

Spent a good night in the trenches last night:

A lot of shell fire came our way and we had orders to put up the white flag and ceasefire at 8 o'clock as soon as the Turks responded and put theirs up.

Our officers and stretcher-bearers went out and helped bury the dead. We had orders not to show ourselves at all, but we had a good look through the loopholes. It seemed funny; not a shot being fired and our men digging there beside the Turks. We had a peaceful meal, the best since we landed.

Our men came back in and the Turks went back. Down came the flags and the firing commenced again straight away. Still, it was a relief to have the smell gone. We put our gas masks away.

There have been instances of similar happenings in wars, as in the Christmas Truce of 1914 that involved British and German fighting men at the Western Front staging an unofficial ceasefire to celebrate Christmas in the No-Man's-Land between the trenches—*with each other!* Even so, Dad's entry reads a bit like a Mel Brooks satire on trench warfare. Here are soldiers from either side of a savage conflict pausing to engage in a burial ritual that bears a definite link to an act of humanity.

The act didn't last. The flags go up. Everyone digs. Everyone buries. The flags come down. Everyone's back in the trenches shooting at each other again. Mel Brooks for sure!

The documentary style of Dad's writing seems a cover-up for what he's feeling. He doesn't mention names. *One of our Generals* is *One of our Generals. Our officers and stretcher-bearers*—anonymous. When men are killed or wounded, they are not named. It's hard to imagine that these men could spend endless hours locked together in anything but a *grand adventure* without some sort of mutual compassion or emotional support. So far, nothing is mentioned. I supposed Dad was speedwriting to save time.

He and his mates in the trenches obeyed orders without question but still found a way to sticky-beak at what was going on with the burial detail.

Loopholes in the trenches were spaces in the sandbag turrets to facilitate protected rifle or machine gunfire. The trenches were hardly the Ritz Hotel, but Hollywood loved putting people like Gary Cooper and Robert Taylor in them, rubbing their faces with fake dirt and scratches then telling them to look pained but stoic when the cameras turned.

In the movies, there's no business like war business. Try *From Here to Eternity; Big box office in 1951.*

The trench dwellers at Anzac Cover were not all 5th Light Horse lads, but a fair number came from early Twentieth Century Queensland in 1915, a place of fresh air, wide-open spaces, uncluttered towns and burgeoning cities not yet in their prime. The trenches would have been more wretched for them, but what do you do when they're all you have? Tough it out and pray for your luck to change. "Life's Lottery." *Play it with your life.*

GALLIPOLI ACCESSORIES: U-BOATS AND AEROPLANES

MAY 25

Had a pretty quiet night last night:

I was out in front of our trenches on patrol and it was raining again. The Turks opened fire on us with a machine gun, but no one was hit. Their bullets were going too high. They should have got the lot of us.

The battleship Triumph was torpedoed and sank just off Gaba Tepe. We could see it plainly from our position on the hill. She sank half an hour after she was hit. We heard there were men saved but the Turks shelled the rescue boats. The guns of the Triumph were firing right up to the time she went down. We don't know how many men went down with her or how many died in the water.

The loss of *HMS Triumph* hit the men hard. My father had an old faded photograph of her, and he spoke about her with the same affection people feel for other people. All kinds of inanimate stuff inspires it—cars, houses, places, anything at all. At the Cove, the object of affection was the *Triumph*. Everyone saw her steaming around every day, up and down all over the place, pinging off at the Turks, dodging the battleships, looking after the Cove like a Guardian Angel. She was tough and proud, and the navy boys on board kept in touch waving and signalling the thumbs-up. She inspired confidence, and she gave the Turks no leeway.

Dad commented. *"We could always rely on her to be around. She came good when we were in a tight spot. You looked out to sea and there she* was. She was a bloody good mate and we missed her."

Triumph played a big part in the April 25 landings at Anzac Cove. Standing offshore in the Aegean Sea in wireless contact with a Sopwith Tabloid biplane in the sky above, she was on the job as defender of the ANZACs. The Turk's prize battleship *Turgut Reis*, anchored in the Dardanelles, four miles away across the narrowest part of the Peninsula had her guns trained on the ANZAC landing, making things rough. *Triumph's* gunfire, guided by the Sopwith pilot, hammered the enemy battleship with such precision that the game was over. *Turgut Reis*, outwitted and badly damaged, limped out of range.

For days after April 25, *Triumph* held her watch-dog position, cruising between Cape Helles and Gaba Tepe, continually shelling the Turkish lines with her ten-inch guns. Protected by torpedo nets and her escort destroyer *HMS Chelmer*, her salvos helped keep the Turks on the hop. Time after time *Triumph* and *Chelmer* saved the day.

Then it happened. One of the U-Boats got lucky and hit her with one torpedo while she was shelling the Turkish lines. She listed badly, and the men on the hill looked on helplessly while she went down; her guns still blazing.

> "They got her with one torpedo. It was awful watching her die like that. I don't mind owning up that I had a tear in my eye and so did most of the other blokes. They got our Guardian Angel, and we had to watch them shelling the rescue boats. It was bloody awful listening to the cries of those sailors in the water but what could we do? It was a sad day."

Over 70 of the *Triumph's* crew drowned. *Chelmer's* lifeboats, plus another two destroyers managed to nose close to the dying ship to save another 500. The sinking was a major blow to the sea-bound protection strategy of the entire fleet, and the men on the Cove hill knew it.

MAY 26

We came out of the trenches last night and into supports and had a good night. Things were

> *pretty quiet in front of our line but there was a lot of rifle fire over the New Zealand trenches on our left. The battleship Majestic was torpedoed, and she sank off Cape Helles at nine o'clock this morning. A Taube flew over our lines today and bombed us but didn't do too much damage. Our planes came on the scene and the Taube cleared out.*

The sinking of *HMS Majestic* was another blow. German U-Boats slithering silently around under the blue waters of the Aegean Sea were not missing a trick. Two prize battleships in two days! The Allied navy commanders were getting edgy, and they began having second thoughts about the effectiveness of their torpedo nets. The U-Boat captains had found a way to get past them or through them, twice. How many more hits would there be? With battleship and destroyer cover from the sea exposed to lucky U-Boats, spirits in Anzac Cove were hardly flying high.

Things were not going well on Gallipoli. The Tommies at Cape Helles were getting nowhere. Every time they made a move to break out, it was stalled, and they continued to be locked down with their backs to the sea. At least supplies of food and ammunition were coming in regularly, and they were holding on in stalemate conditions.

Spring was now in its last gasp and the summer was closing fast.

The sea breezes were warming, and haze from the smokestacks of the battleships hung heavily in the air. As the Middle Eastern summer moved in, The Dardanelles Campaign was beginning to cause serious headaches and sleepless nights in London. Still no talk of the retreat the critics were screaming for, but the decision-makers, whoever they were, wanted none of it. Over the decades this denial has been debated but never fully explained.

All anyone knows is that pleas for a withdrawal in late May or early June were knocked back. The morale of the fighting men was evaporating daily, but the fighting went on.

Now and then there were indications that London may have been getting it together: There were rumours of reinforcements from Egypt; murmurs only. Hopes rose with suggestions that London must have had a trick up its sleeve. Everyone waited. No trick. No treat.

One of the sternest critics of The Dardanelles Campaign was the official Australian war correspondent, Ellis Ashmead-Bartlett, who reported to the *Daily Telegraph* in Sydney. Jaded and frustrated by what he saw as the incompetence of Ian Hamilton, he raged against Gallipoli's military censor, Captain William Maxwell, who repeatedly prevented Ashmead-Bartlett's opinions of Hamilton and his campaign from reaching the London press. Things got worse: Ashmead-Bartlett was on the *Majestic* when she was torpedoed. He survived to recuperate on the island of Imbros where he proceeded to hit the bottle in a big way. His censorship efforts were scuttled by booze and anger, and he allowed his demons to overtake him. With his resolve weakened, William Maxwell was handed the solution to a troublesome problem. He simply drank it away. Who can say what would have happened had Ellis Ashmead-Bartlett kept his head? Had he continued to fight the censorship imposed by Maxwell, who was acting under orders from Ian Hamilton, the war may have taken a different tilt. It was not to be.

The ongoing tragedy was Cape Helles, an overcrowded jumble of men and munitions sitting like a ruptured duck at the southern tip of the Peninsula. Ragged and wretched, close enough for the smell of gunfire to sting the nostrils of the men in Dad's trenches, it was looking more like a lost cause as the days staggered on. To ease the frustration at the Cove, someone somewhere would laugh at a joke, or a wistful voice would sing the chorus of "It's a Long Way to Tipperary." Amazingly enough, another voice or voices would join in:

"Goodbye Piccadilly, Farewell Leicester Square." *Goodbye world and hello Gallipoli.* The gang's all here, so where are the dancing girls singing "Hands, Knees and Boomps-a-Daisy"?

One minor move marginally lifted the flagging spirits of the fighting men:

The Brits loaded four new Sopwith Tabloids onto *HMS Ark Royal*, the Royal Navy's prized aircraft carrier, and sent them to the Greek island of Tenedos.

The planes were equipped with floats to land on water; they weren't armed, they weren't impressive to behold, they weren't big, but they were great on reconnaissance missions; easy for pilots to manoeuvre, and they looked as though they meant business. They were a bit of a novelty in the Middle East in 1915 when airpower was in its infancy and they were freely referred to back then as *the eyes of the air.*

> "Our Sopwiths sounded a bit like the Puffing Billies that cart the sugar cane to the refinery in Bundaberg. They were noisy, and you always knew they were there because you could hear them coughing and wheezing. They could fly low over the Turkish trenches and if they were shot at, they'd fly out of range. Their job was to get a bird's eye view of everything and pass it on."

The Sopwiths were prophetic examples of the air-wars of the future. As the Great War battled on; flying machines signalled the end of trench warfare and mounted combat. They did not cancel out hand-to-hand fighting entirely but experiments with aircraft over the Peninsula, and particularly over the fields of France, were the first steps to the eruption of the air power that dominated the Second World War.

The Allies didn't have the Gallipoli skies to themselves. Both Turks and Germans realised the worth of flying machines, not only for reconnaissance missions. The German model was the Taube, sleek, small, and easy to manoeuvre, with one drawback—bombs carried in the cockpit had to be dropped by hand. With one hand steering the rocking plane, aiming, and dropping a bomb with the other was hit and miss, mostly miss. The Taube Dad writes about had a wobbly go, then took off, chased by a couple of unarmed Sopwiths.

U-Boats were still a threat. After they'd taken out the *Triumph* and the *Majestic*, *Ark Royal* was moved from tiny Tenedos island to the comparative safety of the deep-water bay at Imbros, larger and further away from the Peninsula. Sopwiths, still based on the *Ark Royal*, continued to fly over the Aegean Sea on double missions; U-Boat patrol and reporting on the movements of the enemy. Reconnaissance flights were vital, but it was said that there were not enough of them and that it took too long for reports to reach the right quarters.

MAY 27

> We're still in supports but things are not so quiet today. The rifle fire is very heavy. We lost ten men last night to shell fire. The Turks attacked on our right at daylight this morning but were driven off with heavy losses.

We were up digging a gun road all day with Turks shelling behind our lines. Some of the shells went close but didn't do too much damage.

MAY 28

Went out with a detail on patrol last night and did not feel too safe.

While we were moving close to the ground a Turkish patrol came within a few yards of us. They knew we were out there but looked in the wrong place and didn't see us. We could not attack them because they had twice as many men.

When they finally discovered where we were, we headed back to the trenches fast. Shots were fired but we made it back. When we settled in, we found we were a man short. I went out with three men to look for him and found him dead. We brought him back to our lines just before daylight. One of the three men with me was hit as we got back to the trenches and we took him down to the Dressing Station with the dead man.

MAY 29

Back into the Front Line again at six o'clock last night: We had it pretty quiet.

A patrol made up of one officer, Lieutenant Hanly, and twelve men went out during the night and they were not back by daylight. We think they were either killed or captured as it would be impossible for them to be patrolling in daylight. We looked for bodies between our lines and the Turkish lines but saw nothing. We think the patrol must have been captured. The Turks have been quiet all day.

MAY 30

We are still in the Firing Line. The Turks attacked the 1st Brigade on our left last night but were driven off again. 25 men and two officers went out to try to find Lieutenant Hanly and the missing patrol. They only found Mike Powis who was shot in the knee and lying in a bush all night and most of the day. No trace could be found of any of the other men. All of them, including Lieutenant Hanly must have been killed. The Turkish Patrols are now out with bayonets fixed to their rifles and they drove our search party back.

MAY 31

Came out of the Front Line at daylight this morning:

My mate Sgt. Solling was seriously wounded coming out of the trenches. A shrapnel bullet went through his left arm and into his chest just under his armpit. He looks bad and is hardly able to breathe. I'm taking him down to the Dressing Station as soon as I can, and I hope he'll be all right. They're crowded down there, and he'll be laid up for a while I'd say.

Dad is mentioning names at last! He's feeling the pressure. The good-to-bad-to-worse-and-back-again flow of the battle is getting to him, and things are getting personal. He knew the wounded and missing men. Lieutenant John Hanly, a grazier from Dalby in Queensland was posted as missing and did not survive the patrol referred to. He was officially listed as having been killed, not on May 30 as Dad says, but on June 6; obviously when his body was brought in and identified. Rex Solling, who enlisted on the same day as my father, survived to rise to the rank of Lieutenant. He was treated at one of the tent hospitals on Imbros and was back in the fight by the middle of June.

The wounded Sgt. Michael Powis from Ayr in north Queensland also enlisted on the same day as my father. He recovered on one of the hospital ships and returned a few weeks later. Dad found out he'd been killed in an attack on a Turkish gun battery not long afterwards. Life was cheap on Gallipoli.

Monday, May 31, 1915: My father's twenty-fifth day at Anzac Cove. His diary entries have not missed a day.

> *"I wrote everything down as soon as I could, so I didn't forget anything. I wanted you to know what was happening to change the man I used to be."*

ME GROWING UP

THE DAY MUM TOLD ME Dad had once referred to himself as the "*man I used to be*" I was about to turn twenty-one and my party was on the way. I thought the "*man I used to be*" sounded like a line from a movie and it hit a button! Make no mistake, movies were big in the fifties, and they had an enormous influence on our lives.

Dad had suggested that he was a with a "past" — amnesia maybe? Gregory Peck in *Spellbound*; how good was that? The big hit was *From Here to Eternity,* an over-hyped potboiler about the lead up to the Japanese raid on Pearl Harbor. It had just come out, and if you hadn't seen it, you had nothing to talk about. As a result, all war movies were big: *The Desert Fox, The Rats of Tobruk, The Halls of Montezuma, The Frogmen.*

Guess who hogged the spotlight talking about Gallipoli? I was right on it. I was also growing up. My life was filled with the hunger of youth. I wanted to eat the world. Things were different then; less complicated, less controlled, much easier than they were to become when sophistication took over and people traded their freedoms in exchange for conformity, and bowed to the pressures of their peers and big business.

There were no supermarkets in those days. Mum bought our groceries from the corner shop, and got our fruit and vegetables from a bloke with a truck who rang the front doorbell.

My friends were happy young people; we did happy things. Every day gave us another reason to look for excuses to have fun. Television was still a couple of years away, but morning radio was huge. There were no shock jocks. DJs were real and way-out funny- bright patter, clever comments, and smart put-downs. They played the hits, talked everything up and everybody listened. Talkback came on at 9 o'clock. We were at work by then and it wasn't our scene anyway. We didn't listen at night; we were doing other things and listening to each other.

Television finally hit in the late fifties, a real event. It caught on fast, so fast that in rapid time it closed over sixty per cent of the suburban picture theatres that had done sellout business during the Second World War. Not everyone had TV sets; they were not cheap, and people resisted for a while. In any case, watching the telly was a club thing. We watched in hotel bars or in groups in someone's lounge room where we could ping-off at everything and have fun.

The first big shows to hit Australia were imported: *Hawaiian Eye, 77 Sunset Strip, Wagon Train, Gunsmoke* and *Adventures in Paradise:* No violence. No four-letter cursing. No sex. Cheeky innuendo: Lots of new stars; lots of old ones; glamour to spare; heaps of panel-games and variety shows. Good clean family stuff. If you wanted dirty you could always read *Forever Amber* or *The Sunday Truth*. In Brisbane, that newspaper serialised a sexy French novel called *The Loves of Caroline Cherie,* and turned everyone's Sunday mornings into sweat-shops. Mum thought it was a disgrace; Dad didn't agree, neither did the newspaper. Sales rocketed.

By the mid-sixties, local Aussie product had elbowed into television. The Melbourne-produced Crawford cop shows *Homicide* and *Division Four* took off and paved the way for the local variety and panel shows that made stars of Graham Kennedy, Bert Newton, Don Lone and Digby Wolfe.

In Brisbane, Channel 7 produced a weekly line-up of variety programs that gave television careers to George Wallace Jnr and Eddie Edwards, and kick-started the Bee Gees. Brisbane Channel 9 followed suit, single-handedly launching the mega-money career of Reg Grundy, who took a punt on a slick celebrity panel show called *I've Got a Secret* in 1965. I was a member of the production team. Within a year, that show pumped Reg into the big time of local television. Success had us all walking on air. Reg was no slouch: in no time at all, he was kicking mega-money goals in the United States. His soon-to-be wife was Joy Chambers; beautiful, curvy, and blonde, a Brisbane *Sunday Mail* Sun Girl and a glamour panellist on his Channel 9 games shows. Her sparkle and charisma pumped Reg's ratings into the outer limits, and her hitherto unknown talent for writing has made her a successful novelist.

My father was bewildered by television. He was chuffed that I worked on Reg's shows, and although I knew Gallipoli had never left him, I never lost him. I still went to Dawn Services with him, and he was always interested in what I was doing.

Aussies didn't talk about sex *out loud* in the fifties and sixties. They found nice cosy spots to experiment and learned about it when no one was looking. In the movies, there was a lot of suggestion and innuendo, but sex was pretty tame until Rita

Hayworth hoodwinked the sensors and fired up in *Gilda,* and Marilyn Monroe let loose in *The Seven Year Itch* in Cinemascope. In that flick, it wasn't really sex; it was more like wishful thinking in Technicolor.

Gay was a word that didn't mean what it means today. When MGM launched its big 1948 musical *On the Town,* with Gene Kelly and Frank Sinatra. it was tub-thumped as "Twice as Gay as *Anchors Aweigh"* an earlier musical blockbuster that had also starred them—Gene and Frank in a gay movie? *Come on, guys!*

In the beginning, Australian TV stations signed off at ten p.m. No morning TV. Not yet: *Blissful.* Like all young people growing up, we had off days. We cried sometimes; our hearts broke sometimes. When that happened, we talked to each other instead of pulling down the blinds and moaning, or reaching for a pill or a joint. If things got too bad, we'd go to see Marilyn or James Dean or Marlon Brando or Ingrid Bergman. Movies were movies: Hardly anyone died in car pile-ups or in GCI explosions that wiped out entire city blocks or blew the head off the Statue of Liberty. Our idea of a disaster in the movies was James Dean discovering his mother was a madam in *East of Eden,* or maybe Victor Mature fighting a moth-eaten lion in *Samson and Delilah.*

An even greater downer for all of us was missing out on a ticket to Harry Belafonte's live concert at the Stadium, or not being able to afford a ticket a to the opening night of *My Fair Lady* at Her Majesty's.

The biggest deal in the world was going to a fancy formal ball at Cloudland with Billo Smith's live twelve-piece band and whirling mirror balls: White tuxedos for the guys; glittery Liz Taylor dresses and corsages for the girls. Hot-hot jiving; Foxtrots, Boston Two-Steps, Jazz Waltzing and Gypsy Taps that peaked with show-off skidding for half the length of the ballroom.

No booze; *no booze?* Well—no legal booze. We all broke the rules, and shuffled hip flasks past the doorman, who looked the other way. Who cared? There was no such thing as *drink driving.* If the Boys in Blue caught you wobbling at the wheel, they drove you home.

Drive dry next time, mate . . . Yeah . . . *Thanks, constable.*

If all this sounds too good to be true, it was. Sophistication was Shirley Bassey in sequins and feathers and Bette Davis in *All About Eve.*

It was Crab Thermidor in the Lennons Hotel dining room, flying overseas with BOAC, or sitting in the Members Stand to watch El Khobar win the Brisbane Ten Thousand. When I was one-

and-twenty, dairies, in general, were kind of prissy; they had pretty covers and coloured pages that people filled with all kinds of written fluff:

I'm me, you're you and if we get lucky we can be two.

Back then, that was an everyday diary. Honest. Before I read Dad's diary, I didn't know what to expect, but it was a "diary" after all, and Dad didn't trot it for inspection. When he launched into his wartime anecdotes, he didn't talk about it at all. To tell the truth, I'd forgotten about it until my mother gave it to me the day after he died. I read it through different eyes then. When I read it again with Kitty and listened as she repeated his comments, I instantly realised that the man who wrote it was not the man I grew up with.

In the diary, Dad was the man "*I used to be.*" He had hidden that man away and invented another one to take his place. He had done it so well for so long, that the second man had become real. As the dairy's pages turned, I kept thinking: *How could a man experience the unbelievable, and still be as warm and human as the father I knew? How could that be done? How could he not be spoiled? How could he have lived through the war he wrote about, how could anyone? How could he have written about it so clearly? And the big question: How did he put it all behind him? How?*

I can't remember a time when Dad was in ill health. It came as a shock when he had a heart attack a week or so before he died. He was taken to the Royal Brisbane Hospital and when complications set in, he was moved to the Greenslopes Veteran's Hospital. The attack had been serious, and the diagnosis was not promising. The doctors warned Kitty. The end was coming. She steeled herself. It had taken time, but it was coming all right. She felt it.

I could see it in her eyes. Charlie was packing his kit bag, and he was not going to Gallipoli. *Not this time.*

On his last day on the planet, I sat with him for hours on one of the hospital's sunny verandahs. I had never seen him so calm and peaceful: He knew his life was over. He looked out at the trees and the sky; his mind wandered a bit when he talked quietly to me about what I was doing with my life and whether I loved doing it: Standard chat, both of us talking small talk; saying everything except what needed to be said. Then, in the middle of it all, he came out with this:

> *"When I get to where I'm going, I won't have to think about the trenches anymore."*

It was more like a wish. I asked him what he meant, and he said, *'Gallipoli.'*

I'd never heard him talk too much about the trenches, so I asked him why he was talking about them now. It took him a long time to answer; just when I thought he wasn't going to, he looked right at me and said:

> *"I never told you because the trenches were all about the killing, and I didn't want you to know how much of it I had to do to stay alive."*

I prodded him to tell me more, but he didn't want to. A heavy silence followed. I could see he was upset so I changed the subject. We talked about things I'd forgotten; things we did, where we lived, where we went. It was more small talk, but it was what he wanted. Then, he suddenly took a breath and looked right at me again. His eyes were bright and clear as he fired this sad winning shot: Here's what he said—as close as I remember:

> *"There was only one law on Gallipoli. Kill, or be killed. That was it. It was what we had to do to stay alive. The human values I grew up with lost a bit more of their meaning every time I loaded a gun or pulled a trigger, and every time I did, a little bit of me died. Every time I saw a mate drop, or I carried one, broken and bleeding, to the casualty shelter on the beach, I prayed that one day I'd be able to understand what I'd had to do."*

It was a heavy shot and it hit home. For fifty-three years, he had lived with this terrible guilt. I didn't comment; there was nothing for me to say but I felt for him. On the last day of his life, he'd just said what he'd wanted to say for years, and he'd said it to me because he wanted me to know. He didn't say anything more about the trenches; he knew he didn't have to; he'd given himself a break and set himself free.

We talked on quietly about all sorts of trivial things like the card games we won as partners, and how happy he was to know I'd found a job I honestly loved doing. He said that with a lot of admiration, and added:

"Do you know how many people work at jobs they don't like just for the money or because they're not game to look for something they really like?"

After my mother came to sit with him later that afternoon, I left him to go to work. When I told him goodbye he said:

"Come back tonight when you've stopped making people laugh."

At the time, I was appearing on stage at the *Mark Twain Theatre Restaurant* in Brisbane's Adelaide Street. The building it occupied has long gone but the place was enormously successful in its time. I was cutting it up in a funny Victorian melodrama I'd written called *The Demon Barber of Springhill*'- with seven other actors including Michael Caton, Jane Harders, Brian Blain, Shane Porteous, Henry Crawford, and a kid called Michael Chapman who grew up to co-write Tina Turner's big hit song, *The Best,* and heaps of others. Mike's a millionaire now. Then he was just a kid with ginger hair and freckles.

After the performance that night I went back to the hospital. Dad had died only fifteen minutes before, but I saw him being taken away. When I bent to kiss him, his forehead was already cold, but his face was as calm and as peaceful as it had been when I'd left him. After fifty-three years, the Gallipoli trenches had lost their hold. He had lived in a time of accidental heroes, ordinary blokes who had never expected to be lit by the glow of history or blasted to smithereens by the trumpets of war. His time had long gone for him, but it is still alive in my memories, and it is still alive in the diary that had been his best mate and closest companion in the trenches.

THE OTHER CHARLIE: THE TIMES THAT MELLOWED HIM

THE CHARLIE LORD I KNEW when I was a young man was not gregarious. He kept to himself. He didn't have much to say about the world, and listening wasn't his game. I'm not talking about a perfect specimen. He had his faults, they were in the baggage we all carry through life, but on the credit side, he was straight and direct. When he came to a decision, he rarely changed his mind, a stubborn streak that could be frustrating, but you always knew where you stood with him. Best of all you could trust him. A friend of his once told me, *"They don't make men like him anymore. If they did there'd be no place for them. They wouldn't fit in."*

It sounded like something that would have been said about Humphrey Bogart in *Casablanca*. When I repeated the comment to my father, he gave me a smart reply:

> *"What's so great about not fitting in?' You're a scholar if you don't, and a drongo if you do. Fitting in means you're one of the mob—like a sheep. Who wants to be a sheep?"*

I loved repeating that answer in places like Cloudland Ballroom when the band was playing songs like "Elusive Butterfly" or "*Gentle on My Mind.*" It made people think I was profound, and if you were profound in the sixties you were cooler than Dean Martin. Charlie was an old-fashioned family man; our family was five. Mum, Dad, my two older sisters Dorothy and Lexie, and I was the kid, the one and only son: Five against the world. Dad loved us kids, he adored my mother and she adored him. I never heard them quarrel; it didn't happen in our house: He pulled us into line with a few loud words when he had to, but he and Mum never had words.

Compassion was the gift Gallipoli had given him and he never threw it away. He didn't go out much. One of the things he loved most was staying at home playing Bridge with anyone he could con into a game. At the age of twelve, I was his permanent partner.

He taught me the rules of the game and drilled me on bidding signals and play strategies that mentally connected us from the moment we picked up our cards, to the playing of the last trick. I was the only twelve-year-old Bridge champ in the suburbs of Brisbane; we were big!

> *"Bridge is not a card game,"* said Dad, *"it's a mind game. Dills can't play it properly because they can't keep their minds on the job. Snakes and Ladders is their game. You can play that while you're watching the chooks lay eggs and still win."*

If I made a mistake that wrecked a winning trick, I copped a glare across the table and a detailed de-briefing later. He called it *"keeping your mind on the job."* My father was then in his fifties, but he never seemed old. Not to me. Spencer Tracy was old. Clark Gable was old. Dad was not. In his brighter moments, he was a happy man with an infectious sense of humour that tumbled out in catchy phrases and larrikin observations. He saw the fun in things that other people didn't think were funny. He used colourful expressions: Folks he didn't like were *just like a wagonload of monkeys faced bum outwards*. People who were too thin were *skinny as a kangaroo dog sniffing around a camp oven*. His word for wasting time or sitting around doing nothing was *dinglegarping*. He had great nicknames for his mates.

His name for Mum's favourite sister and her family was *The Porkers*, because they could never resist Mum's pumpkin scones and cakes and apple pies. When he was relaxed, he was nice to be around. If he liked you he didn't have to tell you. When he cared, he cared. I never saw him drunk. Alcohol wasn't one of his things. Roll-your-owns, yes; booze, no. He didn't care if other people drank, but he couldn't wear drunks.

When I staggered home one night at the tender age of nineteen, and did the old one-step-forward-three-steps-back trick on the front steps, he stood watching me. He waited until I made the veranda door, then let me have it:

> *"If you want to drink liquor then learn to hold it like a man. You're no social asset doing the Boston two-step on the front stairs, or lying brainless under someone's table. You're a bloody*

> *disgrace, Drigger. If this is how you want to waste your life, you'll have to change your name."*

He didn't see me boozed again; except at my Twenty-First Birthday party when I trashed the candles with one swinging swipe of the cake knife instead of blowing them out. Dad hid his grin behind his hand. He thought that was pretty spectacular; so did my boozy mates. Kitty didn't. Dad did his Dad-act and said:

> *"You spoiled your mother's night. It might have been funny once but don't try it again. You're supposed to be grown up at twenty-one."*

My mother knew who my father was; she knew all about Gallipoli; knew it all. She stood by him when he needed her, and she put us kids squarely in our places if we ever got too smart-mouthed with him like smart-mouthed kids do. I realise now that what my mother and father had was a perfect love held fast by the glue of empathy, and it saved him, it clouded the guilt and pain of what the war had done to him, and what it had left him with. But the guilt and pain didn't always dim his sparkle. When he turned that on it was a sky show and I often wonder how much brighter it might have been if he hadn't had to live through the one-hundred-and-thirty-days that had forced him to be a cold-blooded killer.

As my father grew older, the world changed. He saw the Australia he'd sailed away from in the Christmas of 1915, grow into a country of ever-expanding opportunities. He watched its development and made sure I understood where he was coming from.

> *"Home is where you live and it's not just a house, it's your country, it belongs to you and everyone who lives in it with you. It's everything you are and everything you want to be. If you don't love your country, you can't know where you came from, and if you don't know where you came from you'll never know where you're going."*

A few of his smart-alec friends were sure he'd borrowed his flowery quote from a desk calendar. He always denied it, but I had my suspicions. One of his mates told him he was an old-fashioned softie with a rose-coloured view of a world that wasn't all that rosy anymore. His mate wasn't getting away with that, Dave put him down.

> *"The world is as rosy as you like, and I didn't get that from a desk calendar. I worked it out on Gallipoli when I thought I was going to be shot. When you think your name is on a bullet, you'd be surprised how rosy you think the world you'll be leaving has been, and how rosy it will be if the bullet misses."*

Australia developed quickly in the wake of the Great War: It was no longer passed off as dumping ground for convicts somewhere in the South Pacific. Its valiant fighting men had shone the spotlight on it, and the world took a second look.

The country's smart men grew rich; entrepreneurs thrived, sporting heroes made headlines: Don Bradman, Norman Von Nida, Lew Hoad, Dawn Fraser, Lionel Rose and Richie Benault. Dad followed their careers, saw the sacrifices they all had to make, whinged a bit when they stumbled and disappointed him, but admired them for what they did and who they were.

We were in Sydney once staying with one of Dad's you-beaut sisters, and he gave me the money to take my rabble-rousing teenage cousin to see the famous Queensland cricketer Don Tallon play at the Sydney Cricket Ground. Instead, we went into town to the beautiful State Theatre to see Rita Hayworth in *Gilda*.

When Dad found the tickets in my pocket, he was so disgusted, he didn't speak to me for two days until his sister bawled him out and called him "old." That did it. Dad was a good sport: Next time he wanted me to see Don Tallon hit a ball, he made sure I went: He took me. He also took me to the races, somewhere most kids didn't go. He had a thing for bluebloods. He didn't bet on them, but he loved them. He could recite the details of every single one of Phar Lap's thirty-seven wins; where and when. He knew Phar Lap meant *"Lightning Flash"* in Siamese, and that the name had nothing to do with laps covered in races, like lots of other people did. Like the rest of the country, he was wrecked when Phar Lap died in the United States.

> *"They said the Yanks could have killed that horse. If they had, it's a wonder it didn't start another war."*

He had other famous bluebloods on his love list: Redcraze, Rising Fast, Kingston Town, the great Queensland champs Gunsynd and Bernborough, and Tulloch; especially Tulloch.

> *"You've heard of Superman. Tulloch is the Super Horse."*

The Brisbane Cup, run in the winter of 1961, was Tulloch's last race. He had been well beaten in the 1960 Melbourne Cup seven months earlier, and rumours hinted that a mystery illness his cost him his winning form. Sharply, the younger horse that had beaten him a few weeks earlier in the 1961 Sydney Cup, was the Brisbane Cup favourite.

As Cup day approached, T.J Smith, Tulloch's trainer, announced that the gutsy galloper's health had improved enough to run in the race. Thirty-three thousand fans hit Eagle Farm, hoping that T.J. had made the right decision about their hero horse.

Sharply may have been the big money favourite but Tulloch owned the hearts of the crowd. He raced evenly in the middle of the field. As expected, Sharply, looking every inch a winner, took the lead after the field entered the long Eagle Farm straight, and set sail for the winning post. But a furlong from home, Tulloch made his bid and the crowd lost it. He unwound a mighty run and charged past his cheeky rival to steal that race for his thirty-sixth win.

The roar of the groupies was the loudest outburst of emotion Eagle Farm had ever heard. I was with Dad at the track that day. At the end of the race, his smile was a neon light. His eyes were shining.

> *"Takes heart to do what that horse just did. You've just seen a real champion and real champions never shy away from a challenge. That's your lesson for today."*

My father saw the Australia he fought for grow up. It was still his country even though the Australia of the fifties and sixties was not the Australia of 1915. He did have a few *beefs*.

He thought the Beatles were *"long-haired dills who sound like they're singing into jam tins."*

He thought Elvis belonged *"in a sideshow in the Woop-Woop Showgrounds where he wouldn't be arrested,"* and that rock 'n' roll was *"idiots delight."*

He couldn't believe people would pay good money to go to a Johnny Ray concert and listen to him *"screaming all night."* He didn't think the Brisbane trams should be done away with because *"that would put too many ratbag drivers on the road."* The trams went anyway.

He had Marlon Brando branded as *"a lout who can't talk properly."* He thought Sydney had become *"too big for its boots,"* and that Twiggy, one of the sixties most famous fashion models *"needed fattening up."*

I took him to see The Magnificent Seven because I thought he'd like it. He said, *"If the horses hadn't been in it, it wouldn't have been worth a razoo."* When Rising Fast was jostled in the straight and didn't win the 1955 Melbourne Cup, Dad said, *"the bloody stewards had blinkers on and should be sacked,"* and he didn't just say it once.

Mum said, *"It's best not to talk about Rising Fast."*

Dad was adamant that the Reg Grundy Games Shows that rated on Brisbane television in the sixties were *"rigged."* I worked on the production team of two of them and Dad was right. They were rigged.

Mum said, *"He's always been hard to fool."*

When Mayor Clem Jones, the man who introduced sewerage to most of outer Brisbane, announced he was going to dig up the inner city's historical King George Square to make way for a multi-level park, Dad was mortified:

"What else would you expect from a bloke whose claim to fame is that he demolished backyard dunnies?"

Mum said, *"It's best not to talk about Clem Jones at the dinner table."*

His very favourite record was the famous tenor Richard Tauber's. "Pedro the Fisherman."

DAD: *"If they played songs like that on the wireless all the time, people would see that Bing Crosby should be selling pies and peas for a living."*

MUM: *"He's got a point."*

When I was still a kid, Dad used to spend a lot of time by himself. I'd see him sitting alone on the verandah of our house or maybe on a seat in the garden under our mango tree; *we always seemed to have one.* He'd sit very still, puffing on a roll-your-own, watching the smoke as it curled into the air. I didn't understand why he'd sometimes cut himself off: Only hours before he'd have been teasing me about missing a hit on a cricket ball or playfully tapping the tip of my nose with the brush when he lathered up to shave. He wielded his dangerous cut-throat razor with great skill, flashing it around like a feathered quill. It was a daily ritual I never tired of watching.

My mother knew to leave him alone when he was quiet; she understood. As I grew up, I learned to leave him alone in quiet times too; it was the unwritten rule of the house.

His is by no means an isolated case; I know that. There are hundreds of thousands of cases just like his; people who suffered the horrors of wars, haunted by memories they could never forget. Most of us have little defence against moments like that, and when they come, we know it's best to wait them out. Some of us can take the kicks; some can't; some let go; some become bitter, cynical, and resentful; others simply find the strength to carry on.

That's what my father did. There were no chips on his shoulders.

His is not the story of a war that should never have been waged. It is not about battles that should never have been fought, or about young lives that should never have been put in harm's way. It is not about politics; it is not about the gold braid of military glory or the mistakes of power-hungry strategists. It is not about opinions or myths. It is not about the envy of hollow men or the greed of despots.

My father pointed no fingers and blamed no one. Dad went to Gallipoli on his own terms, and his story reveals a simple truth: If you're strong enough to believe in what you believe, you'll fight for it. If death becomes a possibility and it's the price your beliefs demand; you face it and do your best to stare it down. The will to live is born in us all, and if there's something to live for, living can keep it alive. It is not always a lonely fight. In the face of death, my father reached for the invisible but invincible support of the people and things he loved, fortifying himself against the dangers that threatened him and the men who fought beside him. He found his own way in the dark and discovered the secret of his own existence.

He did not read it in books, nor did he need to have it explained in grand words by someone who had read it in books. He was not religious, nor was he an atheist, but after Gallipoli, he found no solace in churches or sermons.

He lived with a God of his own; the unfaltering spirit that kept him human in the stinking blood-soaked mud of a country he had never heard of, fighting against men with whom he had no quarrel. Sure, there were times when he felt himself letting go when he wanted to just give in. These were the times when death seemed like heaven, but the unyielding pull of his life brushed his doubts aside every time. He found his soul in the miracle of survival; he lived with death every day in Anzac Cove, and he was one of the chosen few who beat the seemingly impossible odds. Only a handful of his mates survived with him. He lived to wonder why, and I think the wondering led to an understanding of life he may never have otherwise had.

Duty didn't put him on Gallipoli; without love to empower it, duty is little more than a word that fakes excuses and side-steps blame. Dad was there because he thought it was his place. That was his package, all wrapped up in plain paper with a little card that said, *and that's all there is, mate!*

THE GALLIPOLI SUMMER: TURNING UP THE HEAT

WITH THE PASSING OF SPRING, the Gallipoli summer of 1915 finally landed.

Temperatures that year were not the summer temperatures of the United Kingdom. They had teeth—they were to bite the British regiments and bite deep, as Dad knew they would. By contrast, his Queensland mates were ready for it, they could feel it coming, so did the Turkish soldiers who had been familiar with the summers of the north-eastern Mediterranean since they were kids. They had learned how to function when the mercury was rising, and the Turkish masterminds would have been aware of that. In Ottoman circles, the Gallipoli summer of 1915 would have been touted as a secret weapon.

> JUNE 1
>
> *We are still in supports and had a good sleep last night, but we had two officers and three men wounded with shell fire. The B Squadron next to us say it was one of our own shells that burst in amongst them. If we don't soon get reinforcements, we will have to be taken out. It's not good here. We are about 100 men short, but we still have to hold the same amount of line. All the 11th Battalion Infantrymen are worse off than we are, and they need a spell badly but there is no one to take their places.*
>
> JUNE 2
>
> *Went into the Front Line again last night and the Turks shelled us all night. They attacked us and the 11th Battalion next to us at daylight this morning but we drove them off. They got as far as our barbed wire barricades but no further. We gave them a very warm time and it got us a quiet*

day. We never fired a shot after the Turkish attack was repulsed. I have a very bad headache; none of us has had a shave or a change of clothes since we landed and only one wash in the sea. Fresh water is very scarce; hardly any to drink.

JUNE 3

We are still in the Firing Line. The New Zealanders and the 4th Brigade attacked the Turkish trenches at Quinn's Post. The attack made an awful row. It took place at about 10 o'clock and the rifle and machine-gun fire was very heavy. We "stood to" all night and only had a little over an hour's sleep. We had to be ready to go out if the Turks counter-attacked. They did not, and we are not sorry. While I was on watch today a bullet hit the side of the loopholes and a bit of hot lead splashed up and hit me just under the eye. No real damage: We had two men killed; one on the next watch to me.

JUNE 4

We went out of the Firing Line into supports last night and a bullet came into our dugout and went right through my haversack. Luckily, I did not have it on, but it was near enough all right. I am keeping the bullet to send to Kitty. At 8 o'clock this morning, the battleships in the fleet started bombarding Achi Baba. We can see it all quite plainly. I'm glad I'm not a Turk; the noise would deafen anyone as all the land batteries are firing at Achi Baba as well. It's 2 o'clock and nothing can be seen but smoke and dust. The Tommies are attacking Achi Baba. It's 4 o'clock and the battleship bombardment has stopped to let the Tommies through. If they do not take it today, I don't think it will ever be taken.

Two stray bullets; two near misses: Dad was still asking questions years later. He talked about both incidents, and hinted, not flippantly, at the presence of something deeper. One bullet: *coincidence.* Two bullets: *divine intervention?* I asked him if that's what he meant. He was evasive:

> *"That bullet didn't have my name on it. If it had I wouldn't be here, and neither would you. So, if you can work it out you better tell me. There were a lot of prayers going up in that war, and it would be nice to know for sure that one of mine was answered."*

He left it at that, and I didn't argue. Neither, I'll lay odds, did any of my father's mates at Anzac Cove. In the hell pits of Gallipoli, it would have been understandable for men to be wondering about the true meaning of life; to look for answers, and to ask questions about what was happening; and why, with death all around them, some were spared, and others were taken.

It's easy to believe in *a lot of prayers going up*. It's also easy to believe that Dad and his mates were deliberating all kinds of questions that could not be answered by mere mortals. How hard would it have been not to wonder about nasty surprises in tomorrow's kit bag? Kitty didn't get to see the souvenir bullet. It wasn't with Charlie's things when he left Gallipoli, but after the war, she was so intrigued she related his near-miss story to friends, some of whom had occult leanings. When they got hold of the story it became a revelation. *Kitty's husband Charlie* had been the chosen recipient of a miracle; positive proof of something way beyond the ordinary.

MUM: "Who's to say they were wrong?"

DAD: "Some things are better left alone."

What he meant was: *Better left up in the air.* I didn't believe he considered the incident as irrelevant as he pretended. I think he honestly wanted to believe in a miracle, and I bet he did on Gallipoli, too. Kitty's occult team had no doubts. They treated Dad as someone special, and I don't think he minded at all.

JUNE 5

We are still in supports and we have just heard that the Tommies did not take Achi Baba. They lost heavily, and we have been told there were 500 of them buried in one grave. They got into Achi Baba three times but were driven out each time. The news is bad. At least we got down to the beach today for a swim. What a relief.

Casualties in the latest attack on Achi Baba; a rough tally: Turks: 7,000 Tommies: 500 in one grave; possibly more. More dead soldiers to be buried on beaches and in craggy valleys and hills by their comrades in arms; lonely graves marked by crude crosses. After three attempts to break the enemy lines, the latest failure of the British troops to take Achi Baba was another body-blow to the men at Anzac Cove. Achi Baba had held out again; it had been a desperate and bloody battle that the Ottomans had to win, and win they did, at a cost of thousands of Turkish lives, lives that bought the safety of Constantinople. The Tommies lost; the Turks won; they saved their hilly fort, saved their city, and their win cast even darker shadows over Allied plans for Russia and the Middle East. What did George's Boys in London think of that? Still no word of withdrawal!

AT HOME IN ROCKHAMPTON: SINCE THEY WENT AWAY

ON THE *"DOWN UNDER"* SIDE of the world in the far-flung lands of the Antipodes, everyday life went on. As the Gallipoli summer closed on the Dardanelles, the first chilly breath of the 1915 winter blew into Rockhampton. The steam trams continued to run, and the mango trees were setting their flowers. Kids still skipped off to school with books and pencils and fish paste sandwiches packed into leather bags strapped to their backs. The Brisbane trains still arrived with their eagerly awaited newspapers.

News of the Middle East was spasmodic. Uncertain reports from the battle zones painted ugly pictures of a world Rockhampton struggled to understand, while the mysterious shadows of the faraway war dimmed the winter sun shining down on the Tropic of Capricorn.

Churches were filled; candles were lit; prayers were whispered; nights grew longer, and tomorrow's hopes were turning to dust. Australia, once young, innocent, and alive with bright dreams, was discovering what it was like to share the pains of the big wide wonderful world.

The young country had found its colonial feet walking in the footsteps of England. Its buildings aped those of London. The cities and towns of the Antipodes had streets and buildings that bore resemblances to Regent Street, Oxford Street, Grosvenor Square and Park Lane. Even the tiny balconies of inner Sydney's terrace houses, the narrow homes of modest working men, wore decorative British-forged iron lace that had been ballast for convict ships.

The Mother Country connection was easy to identify in the bricks and mortar of the still-growing cities. But behind the doors of the houses where families lived and prayed it was a different story. The people of Australia and New Zealand, who had steadily grown away from the traditions of Great Britain, were now forced to reach for the security of their own identities.

The Australia of 1915 was 14 years on from the country's 1901 Federation and the appointment of John Hope as Aussie

Governor-General Number One. Perhaps for the first time, Australians were proud of who they were, but they were hurting. On the blood-splattered beaches, and in the hills and valleys of death on the Gallipoli Peninsula, their young men were fighting and dying while the Union Jack fluttered over the British trenches at Cape Helles.

Wiser men had cause to wonder about the future of the Mother Country connection. It was still strong but how long would it last? The question was still being asked decades after the Great War ended.

As we sat together reading Dad's diary, my mother's nostalgic backward looks at the wartime scene of 1915 focused on clear recollections of concern that swept through the streets of Rockhampton when the unwelcome news finally filtered through from the war zones of the Middle East. It came via a telegram man on his bike; a knock on the door; the tentative opening of an envelope.

Words nobody wanted to read: *Killed in Action.*

It was a tense time on the Rockhampton homefront. Women caught their breaths when a telegram man appeared. Someone's life would never be the same. Day after day of no personal news, then one day out of the blue, the man on the bike with his telegrams in a leather satchel taking to the streets on missions he didn't want to make. Isolation made everything worse. The waiting was agony; sleepless nights and terrible days; weeping and worry were everywhere. The telegram man's upsetting news was all the worse because it always arrived without warning.

Men of the 5th Light Horse had been killed in the May landings at Anzac Cove. More died in the first Turkish change on the Anzac trenches a little more than two weeks later and the daily tally was mounting. Many of these casualties were Dad's friends, mates from Rockhampton, Barcaldine, and Blackall, who had enlisted when he did. The arrival of the first telegrams relating to the 5th Light Horse on Gallipoli told my mother where my father was. His letters had stopped coming after he left Egypt.

She now knew why. The Middle East was somewhere on the other side of the world and the young men of Rockhampton were dying there. *Killed in Action* were cold words that leaped from the folded pages of official telegrams. What else could be said? The community came together, and people rose to comfort those torn by grief. Official telegrams said nothing about the maimed and broken bodies lying in foreign battlefields or buried in anonymous graves. These were the young men who went away and would never come home, lost to cold and lonely graves in a foreign land that no one knew anything about. It was well that such messages were brief.

At last, Kitty Price knew where Charlie Lord was. She now joined the ranks of the women who did their best to live through another day tormented by anxiety and worry. To ward off the aching uncertainty of her nights, my mother learned to crochet. She turned it into a delicate art by the sheer force or her concentration.

> MUM: *"It eased my mind. The more I worked the easier it got to bear the never-ending worry and the terrible desperation of not knowing."*

She crocheted shawls and scarfs and wove intricate edges on linen handkerchiefs. When the deeper winter nights came to Rockhampton in 1915 she sat for hours with a rug over her legs, a warm shawl over her shoulders, a crochet hook in her hand, balls of fine wool or crochet cotton in a basket beside her and prayed that the man on the bike with the telegrams would never knock on her door.

THE TRENCHES AT ANZAC COVE: THE LONG-HOT SUMMER

ON GALLIPOLI, THE GUNS WERE silent for a while. Achi Baba had survived the latest Allied attack, but the mind-numbing death toll had stunned the Ottoman strategists, and they needed time to recover. The Allies also needed to take another close look at the situation. It was back to Square One for both sides. The men in the trenches at the Cove, uncertain about the next move, sat, waited, and wondered: The stillness gave them time to think and reflect. Dad called it *"a wake-up call."*

> *"We realised, more than ever, that we had to look after each other. If we didn't, who would? We had time to give our mates messages to deliver back home in case we never got back and even joked a bit to keep our spirits up; it wasn't easy but every time I woke up and looked at faces that were still there it made me feel all right. It was even better when one of them smiled back. You knew then that you still had a mate, and for a few seconds the silence made everything seem better."*

JUNE 6

We were shifted around last night to take over a sector of the 9th Battalion trenches. The men we relieved have been there since we landed, and their division is only half strength. They look awful and need a spell badly.

I heard from their adjutant today that no trace of my friend Harry Graham can be found. No one has seen him since the first day and he is posted as missing. I saw Sergeant Knight who told me that the last anyone saw of Harry was on a battleship before the landing. They were the first to land and I think Harry died in the water or on the beach.

JUNE 7

Was out of the trenches on outpost last night: In the Turkish trenches about 100 yards down the line from us we could hear them talking in front of their barbed-wire barricades. We crawled up close to them but saw nothing.

We came back in just before daylight and had a quieter day but lost one man killed by a stray bullet. A Taube bombed us in the afternoon but didn't do much damage. Two guns of the 9th Battalion battery were blown out by a Turkish shell and seven men were killed. Beachy Bill started shelling us this afternoon and we got it pretty bad, but the battleship Lord Nelson came on the scene, fired back, and did a lot of damage to the Turkish lines.

It was on again, *this time with a twist:*
The Turks were playing safe with their infamous Beachy Bill, a mysterious gun battery in the hills not far away to the west of the Cove: Mysterious because of its habit of appearing and disappearing like some trick in a magician's handbook. The Turks, spelling or re-grouping their fighting men, couldn't afford to allow the Cove regiments to take advantage of the lull, so they unveiled their magic machine. Beachy Bill was no weak trick—so named for its habit of picking off swimmers in the water off the Cove beach. It was dangerous and unpredictable, pinging off salvos with no warning. The Cove gun batteries didn't take that lightly and returned fire to no avail. The Bill would stay quiet for a few minutes then open up again, let loose with a few deadly rounds then disappear in a cloud of mist and smoke. This ingenious gun battery also managed to frustrate the British Navy's battleships. One or other of them tried on several occasions to blow Bill off the map. Success eluded the ship's long-range guns every time, and the Bill remained one of The Great War's mysteries. As a secret weapon, it was up with the best. As a killer, it was responsible for hundreds of deaths at Anzac Cove. Now-you-see-me-now-you-

don't was on every page of Big Beachy Bill's rule book; a book that never closed while Dad was on Gallipoli.

Here's one expert's explanation of the Beachy Bill mystery.

It was located near Gaba Tepe, hidden in the hills south-west of the Cove, but it wasn't one gun, it was a collection of guns, one moving up to take the place of a gun taken out by an enemy hit, nothing more than a simple effective trick.

As the lull continued, another Taube pilot tried his luck over the trenches and had to give it up. With the enemy soldiers on a break, enemy fire at the Cove had almost ceased. But in the nearby 9th Battalion trenches, weary and ragged men were copping the brunt of what the enemy bomb experts were throwing around. When Dad and his mates, sent to give them some relief, were on the job, he learned from the 9th Battalion adjutant that his friend, Harry Graham, a 9th Battalion man, had landed with his regiment on April 25, and hadn't been seen since. Harry had been posted as missing and Dad assumed he'd been killed, but that was not confirmed by the 9th's adjutant, who surely would have known. On June 6, six weeks after the first landing, there was still no trace of Harry Graham. Did he just disappear?

He did not: Harry John Graham's cross is in the Lone Pine Memorial on the Peninsula; listed as being killed at Gallipoli on April 25, 1915. Could this mean that records being kept at Anzac Cove were not always current? The subject of Harry Graham didn't come up at home after the war; I only tripped over the mystery when I read the diary. If the Anzac Cove records were not current in Harry's case, could there have been mistakes in other dates, perhaps in the death of Lieutenant Hanly?

Could there have been more errors? If so, could it explain why my father's dates of certain occurrences differ from official records? The question draws attention to the understandable communication problems that existed on Gallipoli. On the subject of the war correspondents, Dad told me that those stationed on the Greek islands gleaned a lot of information from men aboard the supply boats ferrying food, water, and ammunition to the Peninsula beaches.

Was some of this information no more than ferryboat hearsay?

This was 1915, and a terrible war was messing with people's heads. Facts, fiction, and gossip would all have been bubbling away in the same stewpot. There was literally no way of checking anything. There still isn't. Who, in their right mind, would have wanted to be a correspondent in circumstances like this? There was at least one exception. He not only wanted the job; he put his life on the line and dared the devil to report what he saw, first-hand, face-to-face; nothing but the truth.

His name—Charles Bean, a name that conjures up images of a contemporary pop-eyed Brit who makes funnies on TV and in the movies. Gallipoli's Bean was no pop-eyed comic. This amazing Aussie was a hands-on man who preferred to be in the thick of everything. He was on board one of the boats towed into the tangle of the April 25 landing but as destiny would have it, his name was not on any of the bullets that morning. He survived to set himself up for the duration of the war in one of the dusty one-man dugouts in the rocky cliffs of Anzac Cove.

Nuts? *Not the right word:* Dedicated? *He'd have needed to be.* Brave? *You'd have to say so;* Admirable? *Raise your glasses!* A hero? *He may not have looked like one,* but Charlie Bean was no squib and no coward. His fame has outlived him. If you want to be fancy, he was Gallipoli's Clark Kent; *glasses and all!*

> In Dad's words: *"Charlie was a fair dinkum bloke, a bit skinny; with glasses and hair like Ginger Meggs. He was around all the time wearing a funny little hat; we'd see him everywhere writing things down and talking to the officers. We liked him, he'd always crack a joke or two, but he did cause a fuss after the war when he claimed that the papers back home got a lot of his stories wrong."*

Charlie Bean *"caused a fuss"* all right. One of his gripes had to do with his report of the April 25 landing which didn't appear in the Australian press until May 13, well over two weeks after it happened. Charlie also complained that Australian editors favoured the more colourful and dramatic dispatches from British correspondents over his own, referring to his writing as *dull* because he served straight facts instead of tarting them up in the florid language of Fleet Street. It was a point with which he had serious issues.

But in the long term, history has garlanded Charlie Bean, who is revered and respected for professional devotion to the job. He was no-frills-no-fuss, a warts-and-all original, and that can be a problem in the race for fame and glory in the media world, where truth can often be clouded by colourful words and fancy fiction.

If anyone ever wanted to make a rip-roaring, goose-pimpling motion picture about correspondents in the Gallipoli war, Charlie Bean's story would be a bell-ringer!

To be fair to the Gallipoli war correspondents in general, the belief is that they were hampered by the stringent controls imposed on them by the man in charge, Captain William Maxwell, a Dardanelles Committee appointee, who repeatedly clashed with the angry down-to-earth Aussie correspondent, Ellis Ashmead-Bartlett. Maxwell and his backroom boys had the power to edit or rewrite anything that could adversely affect morale at home; or more to the point, cause massive problems for the Georgie Boys who'd had enough on their plates without being hammered by perverse public opinion.

In which case, edited reports could well have been edited again, both in London and Australia to keep morale from falling—*the most favoured excuse.*

In Australia, there could have been another reason for so many conflicting dates and delayed information: Charlie Bean reported for the *Sydney Morning Herald,* but his writings were picked up by other Australian newspapers, and as likely as not edited again to suit the social climate. SMH's opposition was Sydney's *Daily Telegraph*, whose man on the job was none other than Ellis Ashmead-Bartlett, who bleated non-stop that the British Military was forever keeping Australia and New Zealand "in the dark" by withholding vital aspects of the Dardanelles Campaign. Who's to say they did? Who's to say they didn't? The door closed on both questions long ago, and the subject is no longer discussed. The truth is that it can't be discussed because nobody knows what the truth of the Dardanelles Campaign is—or was.

When I went to school, our country's history was an important subject and we were frequently asked to compose essays about historical events of the past. Mine were usually about the Gallipoli War—naturally enough. Gallipoli was a part of my life and I didn't have to do a lot of page-turning to check things out in history books. I got the fair dinkum *duck's guts* when I questioned Dad, or when his closest friends visited our house.

People talked to each other in those days; they didn't sit around texting, nosing other people's business on television talk shows or racing off to shopping centres for coffee and lunch. They were not exposed to media brainwashing and fake news. They were not plonked in front of computers or laptops sending emails or gawking at celebrity sites, and they were not wondering about the latest cash-trapping specials at the supermarket. They looked in the mirror every morning and knew who they were.

They talked for hours in lounge rooms or on verandahs, exchanging views and opinions over cups of tea while they munched on home-made shortbread biscuits or lamingtons made to authentic recipes in the Queensland Country Women's Cookbook. Kitty, a dedicated member of the Queensland Country Women's Association, made the best apple pies and sponge cakes on the planet: best scones too; with Queensland Blue pumpkins if you were lucky. Visitors to our place were in the very best of hands, and they could ask Dad questions while they were munching on Mum's Blue pumpkin scones, *with homemade rosella jam and proper cream.*

Gallipoli survivors were a fast-disappearing race in the fifties and sixties, and people were more curious than ever to know facts first-hand. Enter Dad. His Gallipoli info-line was not always open but when he hit his stride, he didn't waste words. He spoke the way he writes. He was a master at relaying exact conversations word for word, the same every time—often with dodgy accents.

I grew up on his stories and chit-chat; that's where a lot of the comments in this book came from. He was no Peter Sellers, but he could sure hold people's attention, and I always copped great marks for my essays in school. My pretty English teacher read the best ones out to the class. Dad thought that was *great*, but couldn't resist a dig:

> *"Tell your teacher you'll give her Bridge lessons for free if she can teach you to tell the difference between Don Tallon and Rita Hayworth."*

When I read his diary for the first time it brought all those conversations with tea and pumpkin scones back in vivid detail. I also caught on to something else. Charlie Lord, like the military censors, had exercised restraint at his tea-and-biscuit-tell-alls at home. He either left out the diary's ugly bits or played them down. I didn't need to wonder why.

Many returned men in that war didn't like talking about it at all; they preferred to keep it locked away. Dad let some of it out; not all of it, but enough to help people understand just how rotten things had been. He always avoided arguments and lightened up if it all got heavy; if it got too heavy, he clammed up and changed the subject.

CAPE HELLES
The Allied Fort at the southern tip of the Gallipoli Peninsula

Ian Hamilton

THE WAR ROLLS ON: FROM BAD TO BIZARRE

JUNE 8

The Turks kept up heavy fire all night without any damage.

We are very short of water and have not had a wash for over a week. Just hardly enough water to drink, half a bottle for 24 hours and the weather is awful. It's very hot and the flies are very bad. We're getting food of a kind. Sometimes we get cheese and jam but the cheese is too strong to eat and if you try to put the jam on biscuits it is black with flies before you can put it in your mouth. We have only been here a month and a bit, and it has been proper hell, worse than anybody could imagine. If I had not been here, I would not believe it.

JUNE 9

Our outpost was attacked last night, and we lost four men.

Fifty of us went out afterwards but the Turkish patrol met us and tried to draw us into their machine gunfire. We got away just before daylight and things have been pretty quiet since then. But the Tommies are having a terrible time down at Cape Helles.

JUNE 10

Twelve of us were out again last night and we were very nearly all captured.

The Turks attacked us with bayonets. There were about a hundred of them and they tried to cut us off from our Front Line. We held them off with rifle fire and got back into the trenches just in time. Only five of us made it. We tried to bring in a wounded man, but the Turks were right onto us. We had to leave the man. He was in awful pain, shot through the spine and dying. Things were pretty bad all day. Last night there was a big attack on Quinn's Post.

Our troops took a line of Turkish trenches and have held them. We stood to all night ready for a counter-attack, but it didn't come. The Turks kept sending up star shells all night. We have had no water all day but expect to get some tonight. Our clothes are awful. We have not had a change since we got here over a month ago.

The summer peaked.

No let-up: Hard cheese, biscuits, jam, and flies; no picnic: Bayonets and star shells; no water; filthy uniforms, Achi Baba; snipers, lice, bullets, a scorching sun, and more of that bloody Achi Baba. Take time to examine the Dardanelles Campaign: Sooner or later it's a bad dream on a dark night, and there's no waking up. There's not much logic or sense to anything. On the pages of history books, it resembles something Gilbert and Sullivan would have written; a lurid tra-la-lah that reads like a comedy of errors.

Consider the evidence:

Churchill sails his navy into the Narrows of the Dardanelles knowing the waters have been mined, that the eastern seaboard of the Gallipoli Peninsula is lined with gun batteries, and that Çanakkale on the mainland Turkish side of the narrows is a well-armed fortress. *He still does it.*

Ian Hamilton aims thousands of young men at the high rocky cliffs of the eastern seaboard of Gallipoli in boats that must be towed. *They pile up.*

He aims thousands more at Cape Helles in the mistaken belief that the defending Turkish army is a made-up mob of amateurs. *They're not.*

He expects his armies to march across the Peninsula to knock out the Turkish gun batteries guarding the Dardanelles Narrows in one day. *It doesn't happen.*

Cape Helles is a death trap. Anzac Cove is a disaster.

Allied regiments in both places are trapped in abysmal conditions. The death toll is rising day by day. Nothing is going right. Morale is falling alarmingly. The great invasion of the Gallipoli Peninsula was supposed to claim success in one day. *It's lasting weeks.*

As of June 10, 1915, that's how it was. But did anyone guess that it was only the beginning? What Fate had in store for Gallipoli was something else again.

The something was another juggernaut, and it was already gearing up!

In the surrounds of Anzac Cove, a tug of war is going on:

The hot action spots are two trench posts: Quinns and Chathams; they change hands at the drop of a gun.

Quinn's Post; dangerous; one of the most notorious hell holes of the Gallipoli War; the Cove's neighbouring flea pit; but a prize to be captured and held; the strategic brainchild of Major Hugh Quinn, a 15th Battalion officer from Charters Towers in far north Queensland. Hugh and his men dug it out of the hard, unfriendly ground, four days after the first Anzac landing; first one trench, then another, then more and more trenches, until they became a little fort in the ground. Blood, sweat, and tears built it; bullets and bombs protected it.

Hugh, a very bright soldier, knew what he was doing. His post was in the perfect spot to dish it out to the enemy as soon the order to charge across the Peninsula to attack the Dardanelles gun batteries was given.

The Turks were aware of that, and possession of Quinn's Post became an ongoing tug-of-war. Hugh didn't live to see the rewards of his stout efforts; the order to charge the gun batteries was never given but he was spared the disappointment. He lost his life in one of the bloody grabs for his post on Saturday, May 29, 1915.

He went down in his trench, a valiant man among men. In a war that grew heroes like fields grow poppies, he was a hero among heroes; gone, sadly missed, but not forgotten. The post that held his name, no matter who was fighting in it, is Gallipoli history.

Chatham's Post—close to the eastern Peninsula cliff tops, a decent spit south of Anzac Cove. Established by the youthful 5th

Light Horseman, Lieutenant William Chatham. His dig-a-thon was the work of 200 men and 20 overseers who marked out the line of trenches. The English-born William was on the job keeping spirits bolstered while the picks and shovels dug, non-stop. His Post was positioned to protect the Cove from southern enemy raids and to provide a launching point in case of an ANZAC move on the village of Krithia. As such it was a prime target for the Turks, who needed to own it to keep the Cove regiments away from Krithia. If they could take Chatham's and hold it, they'd be able to shove the ANZAC regiments right off the cliffs and into the sea; *hardly impossible!*

William Chatham survived Gallipoli to be wounded in Palestine in 1916. Miraculously, his luck held; he survived Palestine to return to Warwick and to the grazing life that turned him from an ambitious Pom into a dinkum Queenslander.

His legendary Post was close to the Turkish village of Krithia. Krithia protects Achi Baba so the Turks must take the Post and keep the ANZACs out of it.

If they don't; what price Krithia? If Krithia is taken, Achi Baba is next; if Achi Baba falls, the Allies break out of Cape Helles and the Ottomans start waving white flags! The Chathams Tug of War went on and on.

By early June, the Dardanelles Campaign is one impossible mess.

Nobody is winning. Nobody is losing. Both armies are losing men; thousands of them. Heartbreak and death stalk the Gallipoli Peninsula like prowling tigers. The war is a stalemate. The Allies don't know how to break it; the Ottomans do; all they need is to hang on and outwit the enemy. So far, they have been good at both. Why not? Their armies are fighting on familiar territory. Gallipoli is not Piccadilly Circus; it is not Sydney's Martin Place and it is not Rockhampton or Barcaldine; it's where the Turkish soldiers grew up. They know the land; they know the weather. It's summer. It's June. It's hot; it's their kind of weather, they're on home ground.

Nobody can see into the future; nobody knows what it will bring; nobody dares hope. Everybody wants to go home—and the band plays on in the Great Circus of War under the Gallipoli Big Top. It's beyond ridiculous. It's beyond understanding. It is beyond God. It will never be fully understood. Amazingly, in all this mess there was something everyone had forgotten; the something Charlie nailed when he gave Kitty his reason for going to war.

His simple statement, *re-quoted here,* had the bright lights of truth all over it:

> *"No bunch of bullies; no matter how big they are, have the right to take or harm or spoil anything that belongs to anyone else . . . If they do it over there, it won't be long before they'll want to do it here, and if they're big enough they'll try".*

In all the barking and nay-saying that still goes on during debates about the Gallipoli war, there's one more point that's always forgotten and overlooked. Nobody won that war; it was always a jigsaw puzzle. It started as a dream and finished a nightmare. It was never supposed to be the disaster it was. That's its history.

Charlie was right about something else again:

> *If the might of the Ottoman Empire had united with the industrial might of Germany to accomplish what its masterminds had set out to achieve, the story would have had a different ending; everything would have changed. The British Empire and its Allies would have collapsed, and if the British Empire had collapsed, its dominions would have gone down with it. Australia and New Zealand would have been taken over, and the world as they knew it would have ended.*

That's exactly how Dad called it in Rockhampton in 1914, and that's what he was doing on Gallipoli. You talk about champions, this one lived with his beliefs, and he was ready to die to let them live.

To this day, there are unanswered questions.

Was fear of the Empire's fractured destiny if the war had been lost, the reason for the constant denials of an Allied retreat from the Gallipoli Peninsula?

If that retreat had been allowed to happen, would it have been seen as the four feathers of cowardness that could have downgraded the worldly supremacy of the British Empire? Would England have ever been as mighty again?

Has this possibility been allowed to disappear into the mists of over one hundred years? Has it been deliberately covered up, unmentioned and eclipsed by controversy and confusion?

Seen through the eyes of its time, the Dardanelles Campaign was passed off as a noble catastrophe fought to make sure the Union Jack continued to flutter as the only true democratic flag in the world, a world that would have been lost forever had Germany and the Ottoman Empire been victorious.

The British Empire could not afford to lose a war it didn't start. The Muslim-heavy Ottomans and their German allies could not afford to lose the war that could have given them everything. In truth, they overplayed their hands and had too much at stake. "Too much" didn't end with Europe; "too much" was world dominance. They were the architects and kings of the game; anxious for the spoils, and prepared to do anything to win them.

Britain, France, and Russia were not ready for the Great War of 1914-18 but what choice did they have? What choices did Australia and New Zealand have? These countries chose to stand together to take on the German-Ottoman Goliath; *win or lose!* When people look at Gallipoli today, they see it from the distance of decades and the picture is blurred. What they see are the horrors my father wrote about. They are suitably angry and disdainful. They point fingers. They ask questions that can never be answered, so they make up their own answers; answers based on supposition, assumption, or fragments of knowledge.

They critically cluck over what Dad says, but they forget why he was there.

In the long hot summer of 1915, the madness continued. The awful truth is that fighting men on both sides were being sacrificed on the altars of both empires to appease the shameless heavies in charge of one of the most ridiculous war games ever played. Conditions were abominable; humanity was buried in mud or drowned in blood; caring was out the door, the fever and fervour of the useless fighting blinded everyone. Day after day, week after week, dogged acceptance set in. The same-old, same-old took over. Mistakes, cover-ups, and more mistakes! The lone winner was the Grim Reaper, who reaped his harvest while the band played on, *and it was too late to change the tune.*

Logic and reason had flown away from Gallipoli to be lost in confusion, lies and the arrogance of men who looked the other way when they should have been facing the truth while the war dragged on, and they didn't want to know. The end was inevitable.

JUNE 11

We were down on the beach last night on fatigue carrying up ammunitions and water. It is damn hard lugging them up the steep hills, and everyone seems done in. The infantry is worse off, and I wonder how much longer we will have to endure this. All our regiments are only up to half strength, but we still have to hold the same amount of line.

JUNE 12

We surprised the Turks and took some trenches off them last night. We bombed them out after crawling on our hands and knees up to about 100 yards away from them. We only lost three men. The trenches we took were at Chatham's Post. They tried to take them back at daylight this morning, but we drove them off. We have had to dig back to our Front Line, now less than 25 yards away from the Turks.

And then there were The Anzac Bombs:
They were really something; more like comic-book stuff; *Rockfist Rogan* or *Biggles*. They were the stars of the raid on Chatham's, and they were not your everyday bombs: They came not from the sky, not from any fancy munitions factory in Britain or anywhere else. These cheeky little firecrackers were hand-made jam-tin terrors: what you said was what you got.

The recipe: Take a pile of used tins that once held jam the flies paddled about on; pack each one with shrapnel from Turkish bullets and star shells; add a decent serve of dynamite, pack it in tight, shove a long wick deep into the centre of the tin and your firecracker is hot to trot. To initiate the bomb, light the wick, check the fizz, then with your bowling arm poised, flex up a decent serve of muscle power; take aim, hurl the bomb at the target, *and kapow! Stand by for the bim-bam-boom!*

If Guy Fawkes had been on Gallipoli, he'd have been green with envy! *But take good care, lads!* These dodgy grenades did not come with a safety seal. They were A-one dangerous and mightily effective but there were no second chances. Nobody stepped forward to be heralded as the original mastermind of these rogue weapons; they just emerged; motivated by need, ingenuity, and the will to win. Daily jam-tin bomb-making kept the assembly line well supplied. It was as close to a fun job as you'd get on Gallipoli—so long as everybody obeyed the no-smoking rule!

JUNE 12

We are still holding Chatham's Post. We had a lot of star shell fire over us last night and expected the Turks to counter-attack, but they didn't come. They have been bombing us all day and we have lost more men.

JUNE 13

B Squadron relieved us last night at Chatham's Post and we went into reserves for a fair night's rest, the best for some time. We have stayed in reserves all day. Things have been fairly lively all along our lines, a lot of fire on both sides as well as a lot of machine-gun and shell fire.

JUNE 14

We heard the Tommies and the Gurkhas had another go at Achi Baba last night but could not take it and lost very heavily. I wish they'd take it because we cannot do anything until they do. The fire was terrific all night. We had a pretty lively night with plenty of fire over us but not much damage. Things have been quieter all day and we got new clothes. What a relief to be in them.

Dad's new clothes: Can you believe it? After six weeks? Six weeks! The clean clothes he put on in Egypt and wore when he landed at the Cove, went up in smoke and took the lice with them. The new lot arrived in bulk from Egypt via the Greek Islands. They did not come from a department store on Oxford Street, London—they would have been welcome had they come from a second-hand shop in Woolloomooloo, Sydney. They were not custom fits; it wouldn't have meant anything if they had been, everyone had lost so much weight their uniforms hung on them.

> "They were one-size-fits-all. Some of us looked like scarecrows but we didn't give a damn. They felt so good and smelled so good we just didn't care".

Achi Baba rides again! The most talked-about spot on the Peninsula. Its name was synonymous with Allied failure and frustration. In Dad's trenches, it was moaned-down with a groan in every syllable and given the dinky-di Aussie syllable treatment: "*Arrr-chee-bloody-baa-baa!*" The cry never stopped:

"*Take it and let's go home!*" The biggest dream of all! In his lighter moments at home, Dad referred to the Dardanelles conflict as "*The Achi Baba War.*" He was adamant that if the Tommies had been able to take it as planned, the war would have been over in days. On that subject, he was holding forth to someone while I was instructing a young card-mad mate on the secrets of Bridge bidding; an eager beaver named Brian; all keen, all ears. Dad was on about "*The Achi Baba War*" being "a bloody unholy mess." Brian's attention was divided; half-listening to me; half-tuned into to Dad.

A week later I was at a Saturday night party—*if you didn't go to one every week you were a social non-event.* Brian's girlfriend Eve, was there, and she treated me like I'd suddenly turned into Robert Wagner. *Big!* Robert Wagner was a heartthrob! On-screen, he was "*Prince Valiant.*"

> Eve looked at me with Sandra Dee eyes and said:
> "Brian tells me your Dad was in a war with the real Hajji Baba."

It took a while to register. Then I got it: One of the fancy Cinemascope movies of the moment was *The Adventures of Hajji Baba*. Nat King Cole sang the title song and it was way up on the hit parade. So, here's my dear old Dad in a war with the *real Hajji Baba!* How fantastic can it get! I did my best to explain Brian's mistake. Eve was instantly deflated, and my Robert Wagner status died on the spot. You can't win 'em all.

Fifty days since the ANZAC landing at the Cove:

No Allied victories to get too excited about. Two battleships at the bottom of the sea, and the navy brass is worried. The German U-Boats are giving them headaches. The two big ships, *Queen Elizabeth*, and *Ark Royal*—anchored near Imbros are considered safe. Battleships and destroyers everywhere else are on high alert. It's mid-June, and it's still hot!

A few weeks earlier, a disturbing news item had rocketed into the Gallipoli war zone. On Friday, May 7, 1915, the elegant British luxury liner *Lusitania* sank off the coast of Ireland. After explosions on her starboard side, she listed badly and ploughed into the sea, sinking in eighteen minutes, taking over 1100 passengers with her. Few survived to tell the story. *Lusitania* had been hit by a torpedo fired by a German U-Boat! Irish fishermen racing to the rescue of drowning passengers confirmed it. News of the great ship's fate added to the stress of the British Navy in the Aegean Sea. Germany had torpedoed one of the world's high-profile passenger ships and didn't bother denying it. They were at war with Great Britain and they were flexing serious muscle, but the German U-Boat captain who gave the order to fire the torpedo, had made a fatal mistake that would eventually kick Germany's butt!

Many of the Lusitania's passengers were blueblood Americans.

The outcry in the United States, still in shock over the sinking of the *Titanic* three years earlier, tore at America's neutral stand in the war. The word, "A*ction!*" hit the headlines. Demonstrations hit Washington streets. In Europe, there was another cry: "*The Yanks are coming!*" Maybe: *not yet*. A state of urgency hit the Aegean Sea: Primed by the fate of the *Lusitania*, Sopwith pilots revved up their lookouts for sinister shadows beneath the surface of the blue water. Most of the time; nothing. *Baffling*. One of the biggest concerns was the safety of the hospital ships. Germany had torpedoed a luxury liner; would a hospital ship be next? Four of the biggest hospital ships in the Middle East were converted luxury liners—*Lusitania's* sister ships, *Mauritania*, and *Aquitania*, and *Titanic's* sister ships *Britannic* and *Olympic*. Were they safe? No guarantee. Their job: Carrying gravely wounded fighting men back to Britain for high-end medical attention, sometimes to hospitals on Malta.

Hospitals on the Greek island of Imbros and the Egyptian port of Alexandria were serviced by smaller passenger ships; any that could be suitably converted. One of them: *Maheno*, a New Zealand cruise ship that plied the Tasman Sea to Australia through the early years of the Twentieth Century. She was commandeered, painted white with red crosses on her twin smoke-stacks, fitted out as a hospital ship and sent to the Mediterranean. After the war, her cruise ship status was restored but by 1935 she was past her prime. Sold for scrap metal she was being towed to junkyards in

Japan when she was caught in a cyclone off the Queensland seaboard and hurled ashore at Fraser Island off the coast of Hervey Bay. The wreck is still there.

The hospital ship situation in June: *Mauritania and Aquitania*: Safe. *Olympic:* Safe; she was still carrying wounded men to Malta in September. *Britannic*: Safe for the time being, then not so lucky: she hit a mine off the Italian coast and sank in November 1916.

June 1915: Days pass; No more successful U-Boat attacks. A later report claimed that Germany had only sent three U-Boats to the Middle East. The hits on the *Triumph* and *Majestic* were indeed lucky strikes. The truth is that the Aegean Sea was such a churn of activity—boats carrying supplies to the Peninsula non-stop, that they hampered the U-Boat captains trying to zero in on a target. It became impossible to get a clear bearing before firing a torpedo. No more "lucky" strikes. The U-Boats backed off, and the navy breathed a sigh of relief.

Meanwhile, the furore over the *Lusitania's* scuttling refused to go away. After two years of listening to Germany's claims that the ship was carrying munitions to Britain, thus negating her neutrality, US President Woodrow Wilson had enough. Bending to the demands of his passionate citizens, he finally declared war on Germany on Friday, April 6, 1917. In Europe, the cry went up again: "*The Yanks are coming!*" This time they were. Armed to the teeth, whipped into belated vengeance over *Lusitania's* fate, sky-high on patriotic drum-beating, they surged across the Atlantic, combined their might with the depleted ranks of the tired Allies, and pummelled the hell out of anything that got in their way. By the time they'd finished, the Western Front was frazzled, and the Dardanelles Campaign had slipped ungraciously into the lurid pages of history.

But for Dad and his mates at the Cove, all that was far away in the future.

The most extraordinary aberration of the Gallipoli War was its cost, not only in human lives but in day-to-day expenses: Ammunition, hospitals, food, organisation, and strategic plotting in the offices of The Dardanelles Committee in London. As costs soared, men in filthy trenches were short of water and decent food. They were making dodgy bombs out of jam tins. Mail from home came intermittently. Rumours ran amok. Correspondents were hampered at every turn, their stories censored and edited. Officialdom was in chaos. Confusion reigned. Frustrated by vain efforts to get the awful truth into the mainstream, correspondents yelped that Gallipoli was true to its reputation; an unholy bloody circus that was a mistake from the beginning. The yelping did nothing to unravel the ribbons of red tape, an impossible dream. At Anzac Cove, on the beach, barges, and pontoons, in the crude shelters and administration stations, in dugouts and trenches, and despite everything, life went on. The enemy had sprung the trap, and Anzac Cove hung desperately to its craggy prison on the edge of the sea.

The outside world watched and waited; largely unaware of the appalling horrors that stalked the craggy hills and valleys of the Gallipoli Peninsula, while the blood poured every day from the hospital ships into the beautiful blue sea.

JUNE 15

Went into the Front Line again last night and things were lively with bombs all night. We lost more men. The Royal Marine Light Infantry came and relieved us today, so we are going back to reserves tomorrow for a few day's rest. If we could only get some good food, it would not be so bad. We are half-starving; only getting bully beef and hard biscuits and bacon: Have only had bread twice since we landed. Saw one of our boys gave 10 shillings for a tin of milk from one of the supply boats.

Black-Market milk? My father couldn't get over it.

"My mate paid ten-bob for a tin of condensed milk when the basic wage at home was less than twelve-bob a week. We couldn't believe it. We all got a spoonful or two of the milk. Talk about rich: if we'd had any more, we'd have all been sick."

Uplifting news at last: The Royal Marine Light Infantry; the elite fighting force of the British Royal Navy entered the scene! They were a class act, celebrated, awarded, gallant and valiant; written about, and talked about as the inspiration for renowned writers of popular military fiction including A.E.W Mason, the man who penned *The Four Feathers*. The men were noted for their spectacular beards, always worn immaculately trimmed, and brandished with pride. These grandly maned Lion Men were not to be taken lightly. They were resolution-plus, an awesome reputation oozed out of them. They were distinguished and illustrious, and their arrival at the Cove, with buttons polished and beards trimmed, was an event! One of their top brass, a Major-General C D Shute, had done his best in the recent past to cancel their age-old right to wear their beards into battle but after a rowdy debate, he was labelled a bully and growled down. From that moment on he wore the tag, "*Shultz the Hun.*"

Not long after the war, Dad picked up on a chirpy anecdote about Shute that was bandied about by a retired Tommy officer living in Sydney. He had fought alongside the Marines on the Western Front, and his anecdote, freely-aired and justly famous, was a sure-fire showstopper: After inspecting one of the muddy battle-scarred Lion Men trenches at the front in 1916, Major-General C D Shute, ignoring the obvious reasons for the unspeakable conditions and the lack of hygiene, ranted that the men's discipline hardly measured up to exacting RM standards. One of the officers, obviously gifted with literary talent and a sense of humour, penned this reply which was printed out and sung to the tune of a well-known military ditty. Dad memorised it as it was chanted by the Tommy officer. Here's how it went:

> *The General inspecting the trenches exclaimed with a horrified shout,*
> *'I refuse to command a Division that leaves its excreta about.'*
> *But nobody took any notice; no one was prepared to refute,*
> *That the presence of shit was congenial, compared to the presence of Shute,*
> *And certain responsible critics made haste to respond to his words*
> *Observing that his staff of advisors consisted entirely of turds,*
> *For shit may be shot at odd corners and paper supplied there to suit,*
> *But a shit would be shot without mourners if somebody shot that shit Shute.*

Dad couldn't sing a sweet note but every time he warbled that ditty in one of his dodgy accents, he was a star. Each time he burst forth, Mum found an excuse to exit to the kitchen and pull an apron over her head.

The Royal Marines were not exactly strangers on Gallipoli. Four battalions had landed at Cape Helles on April 25. Their losses were heavy and by the time their reinforcements relieved the 5th Light Horsemen on June 15, their numbers had shrunk to less than 130 but they were still a welcome sight; and ready to flex muscle.

Dad referred to them as "*gutsy blokes who all talked like Leslie Howard,*" a compliment. Leslie Howard was the Brit actor who played Ashley Wilkes in *Gone with the Wind*, but he had won Dad's prize as a "great bloke" when he played R.J. Mitchell, the aircraft designer who invented the Spitfire in *The First of the Few*, a British movie about the London blitz in the Second World War. In 1943, Leslie Howard died with 16 others when the DC3 in which he was travelling from Lisbon to Bristol in the UK, was shot down over the Bay of Biscay by a German Luftwaffe pilot. Rumours were rife that the actor was a British agent travelling home with valuable information. The suggestion was never proven. After reading about the tragedy in the newspaper, Dad said the true facts were probably *"covered-up."* As a suspected spy for the three good guys of the war, Churchill, Roosevelt and Stalin, Leslie Howard's death was looked upon as *"inevitable."* Dad was cut-up: *"He played the bloke who invented the Spitfires and they got him for it!"*

JUNE 16

We came out of the Front Line last night, had a sleep and went down to the beach to dig another gun line this morning. The Royal Marines lost Chatham's Post last night when the Turks drove them out. We have been told we have to take it back again and it won't be easy this time. The Turks will be ready for us and they will give us hell. Some mail arrived today, and I got a letter from My Darling. Perhaps the last I will ever get from her if we have to go out tonight and try to take Chatham's Post.

Chatham's Post in another tussle for ownership. After being bombed out by the ANZACs three days before, the Turks regrouped, successfully mounted another attack, and dug in. The Royal Marines were sent in to take it back and lost heavily; *unbelievable!* The Turks knew who they were up against and threw all the men they could at their famous foe. It was an uneven game of numbers and the Turks won the day by stacking the deck. There's no boardroom record of how news of that defeat went down in London, it would not have been saluted. It revealed two things to anyone with a sharp eye.

One: Ottoman defeat in the Dardanelles was still on the top of the Lloyd George list of *things to achieve*. Sending an illustrious outfit like the Royal Marines to Anzac Cove was not like sending a bunch of rug rats to a Teddy Bears' picnic.

Two: The gleeful Turkish defeat of the gallant British regiment no doubt brought out a new Ottoman resolve to win the war against the hated British Empire; and if playing the numbers game could do it, start counting!

Dad's letter from Kitty—*My Darling*! High excitement. He kept the letter. It was in the pocket of his tunic when he was taken to the hospital in Malta. Kitty's letter had promoted his response: '*perhaps the last I will ever get from her.*'

How many letters delivered to Australian fighting men on Gallipoli triggered the same response? How many letters were never opened; letters written to men and boys who would never read them from the grave? Hundreds of messages penned by loving hands and sent with a prayer: '*Bring him home.*' How many moments of hope and comfort did those precious letters deliver? How valuable were words on sheets of paper?

> "*Your father knew my writing,*" said Kitty, "*He told me he just held that letter for a while before he opened it, and didn't remember how many times he read it. He said he had this awful ache, and he just sat down on the ground where he was and closed his eyes. Nobody took any notice. They knew, and they just left him alone.*"

THE HOSPITAL SHIPS AND THE ANGELS OF MERCY

THE VANISHING ACT PULLED BY the U-Boat captains blew winds of relief over the decks of the hospital ships. The compassionate rule of The Great War was supposedly understood on both sides. Hospital ships: Neutral. No bombs. No bullets. No torpedoes. But there were always doubts. The Dardanelles Campaign wasn't the place for rules; they were broken all the time. There was anxiety. No one knew for sure about anything. One of the Greeks who piloted the supply boats was a young man named Costas. My father got to know him when he took delivery of water and ammunition.

The young Greek became Dad's link to the outside world; a world that was fast becoming a memory. When the number of wounded men at the Cove Dressing Station exceeded limits, Costas was called on to pilot the transfer boats to the hospital ships at sea, or to the tent hospitals on the islands of Lemnos and Imbros. He willingly did what he was called to do, and although he was a young man, he was conditioned. He had a reservoir of tolerance for the barbs of war, but there were times when his reservoir threatened to run dry. He told Dad he thought about saying no to the hospital transfer boats, but never did; he carried on out of respect for the nurses.

According to Costas, more than six hundred wounded men had been taken to one hospital ship after the Anzac Cove landing. That was just the start of a terrible tide of broken men so badly torn and battered they could hardly hope to mend, even if they managed to survive. When summer came, the heat made it worse. Wounded men on stretchers squinting into the sun; once bright-eyed boys with staring eyes dripping blood; broken young men who could never be fathers; some who would never see again; some with injuries too shocking to describe. The hospital ships, equipped with limited numbers of beds, ferried the worst cases to the Greek island tent hospitals, where nurses were faced with the unimaginable tasks of caring for the wounded in conditions best described as adequate. Under constant stress, they worked long hours without sleep, pushed to the very limits of their profession.

These women were the unsung angels of the Aegean. That they functioned at all was amazing; that they functioned so well was beyond praise. They fit into the Anzac Story in chapters written in agony and pain—long hours numbed by heartache and terrible frustration; the sights they saw and the things they had to do etched forever in their minds; never to be rationalised or fully accepted. Bravery and courage did not begin and end on the beaches or in the trenches on Gallipoli.

> COSTAS: *"We don't know how they keep on. No one does. We see them. They smile at us. They take the men and never turn away. This is a terrible war and I want it to end. I want it for my family, but I want it to end for the nurses."*

SOMETHING OUT OF THE WRECK: A MOVE TO ACTION?

JUNE 17

We are still in reserves. We did not have to go out last night to re-take Chatham's Post. They may leave it for a few days. We have had a spell and have done nothing all day. We heard the New Zealanders took some Turkish trenches last night way up near Hill 971 and they have held on to them. I think we must be going to attack somewhere too as they seem to be saving us for something. There was plenty of red and gold braid with maps around our way and we are wondering where they are planning to send us.

    Hill 971: Koja Chemen Tepe. The highest point of the range that ran north-northwest of Anzac Cove. A short five miles to the east lie the Dardanelles. Due east is Suvla Bay, beautiful and peaceful, still seven weeks away from its part in the war. Hill 971 was a prize possession with a dress circle view of the Cove, Lone Pine and Quinn's Post. The Turks had tricked it up a bit with underground restrooms for its keepers. It had to be protected and held fast at all costs. Because of its position, the Allies wanted it.
    The Kiwis had put the moves on it, and they had grabbed the line of enemy trenches guarding it, a decent, if tenuous win, but they were not uncorking the champagne. Water would have been an acceptable substitute if they'd had any.
    At the Cove, there had been a raid of a different kind. Allied red and gold braid with maps, *a meeting of the military minds*. Dad had it pegged as a strategic move of some kind for the ANZACs, and nobody had to be a genius to work that out. The lads in the trenches sat up and took notice; any kind of move was better than no move. Action at last? Finally, an attack on the Dardanelles gun batteries? *Wishing and hoping!*

JUNE 18

Went back into our old Front Line today: There has been plenty of shell fire from the Second Battalion on our left. They lost heavily, and we lost another man.

JUNE 19

We are still in the Firing Line. The 11th Battalion was attacked last night and lost some trenches, but we joined in and helped take them back after a stiff bayonet fight. The Turkish patrol crawled right up to our barbed wire. I was on watch and spotted them, so we bombed them and wounded three and killed one. We went out and brought the wounded men in. We did our best to treat them, but they died before morning and we buried them.

JUNE 20

Out on patrol again last night and we captured two Turkish snipers, brought them in and handed them over to Brigade Headquarters. One had about 2,000 rounds of ammunition and enough food to do him for a week. His hat and rifle were painted green. God knows how many he shot before we got him. He was up a tree when we found him and after we handed him over, we went out again. We were chased in by a Turkish patrol and one of our men was wounded. We stayed out and tried to bring him in, but the rifle fire was too hot. We left him and had to go out to get him later. He died this morning. My tunic is covered in blood from carrying him. I suppose my turn will come one of these nights. My luck can't last.

The 11th Battalion: The pride of Western Australia: Anzac Cove originals. They landed on April 25; helped dig the trenches; and helped hold them; they had copped it hard, but they were still in the game. They didn't know it in June, but the history books were waiting for them at Lone Pine.

The pages were already turning.

My luck can't last.

He wrote it again. Twice my father wondered about the possibility of not surviving. Every man in his regiment would have wondered about it too. The Turkish soldiers, closer to their hills of home, appeared to be better off. The captured sniper had enough food for a week, unheard of at the Cove. A well-fed Turkish sniper—no sight for sore eyes; not for thirsty underfed Aussie soldiers in blood-stained tunics; the other side of the coin. Even worse. This sniper had been sitting up a tree, camouflaged in a green hat with his green-painted rifle and an unlimited supply of bullets:

> DAD: *God knows how many men he shot before we got him.*

How could anyone at the Cove think about that without running amok? Nobody did. What good would it have done? War is war. Everyone in the same war: Aussies, Kiwis, Tommies, Scots, Frogs, Gurkhas, Royal Marines, Indians, Nurses, Sailors, Officers, Turks, plus two unwanted hangers-on:

The Grim Reaper and Fate: *Who invited them?*

The Twentieth Century was off to an uncivilised start that was shaping up to get even worse.

JUNE 21

> *Out of the Firing Line and into supports last night. The Turks were firing all night. We had to stand to all night, but they never came: Wrote a field card to my mother and My Darling today. I wonder if I will ever see them again. I will never forget the last time I saw them. It only seems like yesterday. I would give worlds to see them again. It rained just a little this afternoon and it is very hot.*

One of the saddest set of words in my father's diary:

> *I would give worlds to see them again. It only seems like yesterday.*

An expression of longing for home and the people who lived there: A man's heart close to breaking. It's very hot and it's raining *just a little.*

What if I die tomorrow? Thoughts of home were written by my dad, pen to paper on Monday, June 21, 1915, when the sun was poised to enter the constellation of Cancer. Dad knew little about astrology; it wasn't part of his world. The idea that planets twirling around the sun could affect anyone's life may have been beyond his reasoning. I mentioned what Dad had written to a friend of mine, Cynthia Staight, who penned an astrology column for a prominent New York newspaper during World War II when her husband was in the Office of Strategic Services. She was adamant that my father's words had an astrological connection:

> *"His birth sign is Aries; his ruling planet is the Sun, and in the northern hemisphere the Sun was entering the first degree of Cancer, the sign of the home, the mother, and the emotional security of deep affection. Your father may not have known it, but the influence of Cancer was strong that day; and unconsciously or not, he felt it."*

In the words of non-believers, Astrology is mumbo jumbo: *that's been said and said again*, but never by my friend Cynthia. She'd been right so many times about so many things that I didn't argue. Astrology was her world, and she lived in it with calm confidence and heaps of evidence to back her up. She said there was no doubt that Dad wrote what his heart felt that day. As the wave of loneliness swept over him, all he had to look forward to, was another day of battle and another night of wondering, while up front in his mind, was a wistful wish to be home. He didn't ever hear Cynthia's interpretation of what he wrote but I did mention astrology to him once. All he said was:

> *"I don't think anyone knows too much about anything."*

JUNE 22

> *Back in the Firing Line last night: Very heavy rifle fire at Cape Helles and star shells as well. It was pretty quiet on out front all night but a lot more*

firing at Cape Helles today. A lot of men were killed and wounded down on their beach. We got a fair amount of shell fire over us as well. We got no water all day.

Star shells: apparently the enemy had a limitless supply of these deadly incendiaries which erupted in pretty fireworks when they exploded. The constant bombardment would have been an effective block for sleep at any time; anywhere. In the Cove trenches, men tried catching shuteye with their heads covered against the staccato glare. Not much point. The weather was too hot, it was too hard to breathe, and they could still hear the explosions.

Forget it!

Seven weeks had passed since my father landed on the Peninsula and nothing much had changed in the Allied hot spots of Anzac Cove or Cape Helles, but the Turks, ever conscious of the importance of the village of Krithia, the guardian of Achi Baba, had recently strengthened its defences to cope with an Allied breakout; if and when one ever came.

The wily Ottomans were blessed with a couple of awesome secret weapons, namely Mustafa Kemal, an ingenious Turkish military brain, and the German mastermind, Otto Liman von Sanders, a couple of major league power players; clever, cunning, alert, and observant. They lived in each other's heads; nothing got past them, and they made sure nothing would. Ever since this pair of war wizards had sent Churchill's fleet skulking out of the Dardanelles, they had the measure of every move the Allies made; second-guessing strategies and trumping the blunders of the Allied leaders.

With these two in cahoots, the Turks had the perfect dynamic duo!

The Brits on the Peninsula had no such luck. In London, the Middle East was beginning to look like a candidate for unpleasant newspaper headline bait, with Lloyd George, Ian Hamilton, and Winston Churchill, the Big Three, neatly threaded on the hook. Lloyd George had the support of the London *Times* and the *Daily Mail*, but the barking dogs of Fleet Street were perfidious by nature. They could turn as fast as it takes to write a negative story.

It didn't happen.

The Big Three were saved from Fleet Street's sword when the Military Intelligence heavies in the Middle East put restrictions on copy filed by the war correspondents. Few negative stories ever left Gallipoli's heavily censored war zone; therefore, Lloyd George in particular, managed to successfully dodge the barbs that could have been thrown at him. In June 1916, he was made Secretary of State for War, and six months later he became Prime Minister. There he stayed until 1922: *Who dares wins.*

But suppose Fleet Street had exposed Lloyd George's mistakes, forcing the dismissal of Churchill and Hamilton and their cronies. Suppose they had all been replaced by someone of the calibre of Lieutenant General Sir William Birdwood, whose reputation as a military man with brains and knowhow; and as an officer and a gentleman, had earned him the admiration and respect of the fighting men who knew him. If that had eventuated, would the outcome of the Dardanelles Campaign have been a different story?

> *"We all thought things had to be going wrong at the top, and we were all cheering for someone like The Boss to step in and put things right, but it was too much of a puzzle for me and everyone else. We weren't asked for our opinions, we simply had to take what we were given."*

Sir William Birdwood aka The Boss, was born in India. He was fifty years old in 1915. After a stint in the Royal Scots Fusiliers, he had transferred to the British Indian Army, serving with the famous Bengal Lancers on the North-West Frontier; a hard-yards assignment. Even so, he was rubbished to bits by his British military critics and enemies, but his Military CV had *dazzling* written all over it. No stranger to the tempestuous and unpredictable military churn of Asia Minor, he was at home in the Middle East, and equally familiar with the political climates of Palestine and Egypt. He'd been General Lord Kitchener's military secretary in India; an assignment that tested his patience and ingenuity. When he came through with flying colours on everything he was given, Kitchener selected him to train the original ANZAC regiments at Maadi for the April 25 landings on Gallipoli.

He was with them when they went ashore, staying on to give moral support, and helping to establish a foothold on the beach while enemy guns barked, and bullets flew around like fireflies in the spring. For that, he was hailed as a man among men. He was a champion swimmer, often braving the Turkish snipers to dive off the wobbly Cove pontoons into the deep water to cool off.

When he was hit in the forehead by a sniper bullet, he refused to leave his post. Result: More waves of admiration from the rank and file. There were very few military icons on the Gallipoli Peninsula. Dad listed The Boss as one of them.

JUNE 23

We are still in the Front Line and there was very heavy rifle fire over on our left last night. There was an attack somewhere near us last night, but we have not heard any results yet. We were out on patrol again but were driven in by machine-gun fire at 11 o'clock and didn't go out again as the fire was too heavy. We got a little water this morning.

JUNE 24

Came out of the trenches late last night and went into reserves. We were relieved by the 6th Light Horse and things have been rather quiet all night: Nothing doing all day.

The 6th Light Horse—the regiment from New South Wales. The men sailed from Australia on the *Persic* with my father and had trained with him in the Egyptian desert. The men of the 6th were attached to the First Australian Infantry Division and they were sent to Gallipoli on the *Lützow* with Dad and his mates. Their trenches at Anzac Cove were close to Dad's, *and here's a funny bit:*

In 1939, when Australian filmmaker Charles Chauvel was making one of Charlie's favourite films, *Forty Thousand Horsemen*, he shot the desert action sequences in the sandhills of Cronulla Beach south of Sydney.

The horsemen he used for those sequences were from the 6th Light Horse. When Dad saw the film. he announced that he recognised several of the men from Gallipoli on the screen. His friends were mightily impressed, *at first*. Then they did their arithmetic. The horsemen on the screen were in their twenties. In 1915, they would have been toddlers! The kids at my school never twigged, and took Dad at his word. They weren't too good at arithmetic at all; come to think of it, not many of us were.

For the record: *Forty Thousand Horsemen* featured the daring cavalry charge of the Australian Light Horse on the Turkish occupied town of Beersheba on the Palestine Front in 1917. The Australian film industry was young and spunky at the time of shooting, and the movie's action scenes were stirring stuff. The stars of the film were iconic Aussie actors Chips Rafferty and Grant Taylor—father of Rod Taylor, the hunky Aussie who made it big in Hollywood in *The Birds, Hotel, The VIPs.* and *The Glass Bottom Boat,* romancing *Tippi Hedren, Catherine Spaak, Maggie Smith, and Doris Day.*

Rod's best trick: He thumbed his nose at Hollywood's honky-tonk and always came across as an Aussie, even when he wasn't supposed to be (*all of the above, except The VIPs*).

JUNE 25

Still in reserves and having a little spell but the worst of it is we have to stand to in full battle dress from 8 a.m. till 4 p.m. We are in dugouts, it is very hot, and we are near a gun battery where we can expect to get a lot of shell fire.

JUNE 26

Still in reserves but we were carrying up heavy gun shells from the beach until 2 o'clock this morning but have not done too much today. We went down to the beach for a swim this afternoon, but things have not been too quiet up in the Firing Line today. Plenty of fire on both sides: the Gurkha divisions lost a lot of men to shell fire.

William Birdwood
'The Boss'

ANZAC COVE when Dad landed in May 1915

THE HOPED-FOR MOVE: DANTE'S INFERNO

FOR OVER TEN DAYS, WORD had been all over the Cove Grapevine that something was on the cards. Speculation was rife; everything from a load of reinforcements to the prayed-for retreat. Everyone had a stab; no one knew. The jokers were betting on a decent feed—a banquet of seafood with Italian wine and Greek biscuits. That scored a few laughs. Speculation continued.

> JUNE 27
>
> *We have done nothing all night and had a good sleep and we have done nothing all day. We had General Birdwood for a visit today and some of the men say they heard him mention that the Royal Scots were going to attack Krithia tomorrow and we would be expected to take the Turkish trenches in front of us.*

Krithia: Was that the something on the cards or just Grapevine gossip? It wasn't gossip! Krithia it was, in which case, the something had to be big!
Yes! Excitement was everywhere! If Krithia is taken, Achi Baba is next! At long last: We're in with a chance!
The Royal Scots, Edinburgh legends, had a Military history dating back to 1633, when James II was on the throne of England. The 29th Division of the famed Scots regiment was formed early in 1915 specifically for action on the French Front. Like Dad's 5th Light Horse, orders were changed when the Gallipoli campaign ran into trouble, and The Royal Scots were sent instead to Cape Helles.
Shocked by what the men saw there, they nevertheless dug in. Boss Birdwood rescued them, deploying them to the Cove when he was preparing for the Krithia strategy. He was, after all, an *old boy* of the Royal Scots Fusiliers, and he needed all the battle-savvy he could lay his hands on.

What was planned for Krithia was heavy; a combined offensive designed to pelt the Ottoman-held outpost with a major force of arms that included the Indian Brigade and a battalion of Scottish Rifles based at Cape Helles.

The Royal Scots and ANZACs were added for extra clout!

The strategy: The Scottish Rifles were to attack Krithia from the south along Fir Tree Spur, which ran parallel to the eastern seaboard of the Peninsula, south-west of Anzac Cove. The Royal Scots and five ANZAC battalions were to move in from the east of Fir Tree Spur across nearby Gully Ravine, several due south of the Cove, with the Indian Brigade backing them up.

Krithia sat slap-bang in the middle of the Peninsula, due north of Cape Helles, with Achi Baba to its north-west. The lay of the land favoured the Allies. The plan was to knock out the eastern Turkish trenches protecting Krithia and advance on the defenceless Achi Baba.

It was a tough ask!

Boss Birdwood knew it, as did every other officer involved. But as usual on Gallipoli, there was a loose page on the blueprint. The Supreme Commander of the offensive was not Birdwood, but Lieutenant General Sir Aylmer Hunter-Weston, the dapper British toff in charge of Cape Helles. The disturbing question: was Aylmer Hunter-Weston a match for the Ottoman titans, Mustafa Kemal, and Liman von Sanders? The question hung in the air. There was no concrete answer, but in the minds of the nay-sayers, Hunter-Weston did not have the clout for the job!

At the Cove, Krithia was on everyone's lips, in every man's thoughts. The lads knew where it was and what it was; the guardian of Achi Baba; so far invincible; *maybe not this time*. They knew an attack on Krithia would be defended to the last man by the Ottoman Army. Trepidation was in the air, but it was tempered by knowledge that The Boss's Royal Scots were the ANZAC's comrades in arms.

The day dawned—bright, clear, and hot; ridiculously hot. Dad's Cove regiments prepared for the 7-mile trek to Gully Ravine. They were steeled and ready.

JUNE 28

> *Had a good night's sleep last night and things were a bit quieter today; at 10 o'clock we got our water bottles filled. The battleships are bombarding the Turkish trenches at Krithia. At*

12 0'clock we heard the Royal Scots were attacking on land. We were all fall-in and every man was told to get his 250 rounds of ammunition and rations for a very hot day. We all got a white patch to sew on our backs to make us stand out from the Turks. Our batteries and machine guns opened up a terrific fire on the Turkish trenches. At half-past one, we all filed into the Front Line to go over the top when we got our orders. The 7th Light Horse was to attack on our left; the 9th Battalion on their left and the 10th and 11th Battalions further down. It was awful waiting. The Turks were only 80 yards away. We had orders to wait for three blasts of the whistle. Just a few minutes before we went over our gun batteries stopped and lengthened their range. We got our orders, and over we went. Men started falling all over the place, but we kept going and reached the first Turkish trench. I had my water bottle shot off before I got very far and just as we reached the first trench a Turk fired straight at me, blew the side of my hat away, grazed the side of my face and cut my chin strap off.

We had a pretty stiff bayonet fight then went onto the next trench and took it.

My rifle was scorching hot from firing. I could hardly hold it. We lost a lot of men going across no-mans-land. After roll call, only 47 of us answered out of 270; two squadrons of us. The 9th Battalion lost 180 men out of one company. There were 200 lost from the 11th Battalion. We got a squadron to reinforce us and we are still holding what we took.

It is awful in these trenches; dead and wounded and broken bayonets and blood all over the place. I went out and was carrying a wounded man back under fire all the time. How there are so many of us still alive I don't know. But the trenches must be held now and if we don't get

> *some help our line is too thin and we won't be able to hold it.*
>
> *We have heard the Royal Scots could not get what they went out for and they have lost heavily. I will never forget today. There are none of us with any water left and we don't see any chances of getting any.*

Dad's words need no embellishment. Imagination is enough but reports of yelling and screaming—the deadly clash of the bayonets, sickening sounds of connecting blades, gasps and cries of the wounded, and the constant *crackle* and *rat-a-tat-tat* of gunfire add to what my father's words don't supply. His comment is on the money:

> *How there are so many of us still alive I don't know.*

Forty-seven survivors out of two-hundred-and-seventy! A day of violent death!

JUNE 29

> *We have held the Turkish trenches all night and they have been shelling us and bombing us, but they did not attack. If they come in force, they will beat us and drive us out. They have been shelling us all day and we have had no water and nothing much to eat. We have bully beef and biscuits, but I don't feel a bit hungry. I am very tired and sleepy. We have been standing to all night and all day.*

JUNE 30

> *We are still holding our new line. The Turks kept up a very heavy fire all night and they keep bombing us. We have had no water yet and no sleep since we took their trenches. Things are very bad. The dead men smell something terrible and they are just lying out there because we have not had time to bury them yet. We had to move the*

dead Turks out of their trenches as we could not bury them either. I wonder how much longer we can last. The ones who got hit today were lucky. They did not have to go through this.

A low point in Dad's life: *The death wish.* Understandable. How much of this can a man take? Look around. Who's not there anymore? Who won't be there after next time? For two-hundred-and-twenty-two of his mates, the dawn of June 28, 1915, was their last sunrise. In the great lottery of life, their numbers came up. It would have been natural to think about who was in charge of the wheel of fortune, and whose giant hand was spinning it.

When do I get hit? The battle was officially recorded as a victory for the Allies, but the cost of life blew minds to pieces: Allies: 3,800. Turks: 6,000. The body count changes, depending on which account is read, but the numbers listed here are Dad's and considered correct; give or take.

DAD: *I will never forget today.*

History didn't forget either: When the Battle of Gully Ravine went under the microscope, several issues were debated. Aylmer Hunter-Weston had been commander in charge of Cape Helles from the outset. Prominent military men had fingered him for the failure of previous attempts to take Achi Baba and he was in their sights again. Gully Ravine may have been hailed as an Allied victory, but Hunter-Weston copped a critical lambast for sending regiments of young Scottish Rifles charging too soon into the machine-gun fire of the waiting enemy along Fir Tree Spur; an almost total wipe out.

The battle heralded the man's decline in health and contributed to his weakening performance at Cape Helles. Correspondents noted that officers under his control eventually refused to take his orders because he was suffering from "*sunstroke*;" a polite way of saying he'd "*lost his marbles.*" Aylmer Hunter-Weston was retired from his post on July 23 and bundled back to Britain. Too late.

What's this? Another blundering CEO; another threat to Lloyd George's place on the Empire pedestal? *Is Gallipoli the land of the high-end losers?* One thing for sure: Those questions were not asked in the London *Times*. Neither were the unvarnished facts of the Battle of Gully Ravine fully reported Down Under; not until the war was over. In the rapidly filling book of Gallipoli bloodbaths, it was just another chapter. Our favourite Aussie correspondent, Charles Bean, was on the spot as usual; he knew all about it and wrote the truth of it, but because his matter-of-fact stories were not in favour with Australian news editors, his Gully Ravine reports were clipped and edited; probably just as well. What the home front didn't know couldn't hurt them.

> DAD: *"The newspapers at home did everyone a favour by not printing all of Charlie Bean's account of that bloody fight. It wouldn't have done anybody any good to know what really happened. We all knew, and we've spent the rest of our lives trying to get it out of our heads."*

There is no record of what *"knowing it all"* would have done to the Australian homefront while the war was still raging. Did anyone at home need to know how many young men were in the slaughter yard of Gully Ravine? Did they need to know how many nurses on the hospital ships were robbed of their chances to live normal lives, or how many lonely unmarked graves littered the hills and valleys of the Peninsula? Did they need a headcount of the women at home who fell prone to the long days and nights of worry that turned to unbearable pain with the arrival of a telegram man on his bike or the sound of the postman's whistle? Did they need to know how many human beings were living through heartache without really living at all?

The war was dragging on and on, and at home, it was getting harder to find out what was happening in the Dardanelles after months of conflicting reports. The homefront came to know soon enough. *In this instance—bully for censorship!*

JULY 1

> *We were relieved last night at 10 o'clock. Brigade Headquarters sent word to General Headquarters that the 5th light Horse cannot hold out any longer and will expire if not relieved by 10 o'clock tonight. So the 6th Light Horse got water for the first time since the attack started. It made us sick, so they mixed it with rum and only gave us a little, but we had a good sleep last night. Everyone looks like beasts and not like men at all. I hoped*

I'd be shot so I won't have to go through all that again and everyone feels the same.

JULY 2

We have been out of the trenches since we were relieved and look a sorry lot. I don't know what they will do with us as we are not strong enough to hold a line anymore. Now not two months here and more than half the regiment wiped out. I wonder if we will ever get any reinforcements. We have heard that the 2nd Division arrived in Egypt and will soon be coming over here. If we're lucky we should get a spell then.

Following is an extraction from an official Army Corps Order dated June 29, 1915. I don't want to comment because I find it difficult, and I'll say no more.

The Army Corps Commander regrets the casualties that took place in the 5th and 7th Regiments of Light Horse and the 9th and 11th Battalions, which were unavoidable, and which must always be expected when we undertake such operations. The Corps Commander is quite sure that the Commander-in-Chief will be more than satisfied with the way in which the Army Corps carried out his wishes, and General Birdwood wishes to convey his grateful thanks to the troops for their excellent work.

Dad kept a written copy of that message. He trotted it out one day when the Battle of Gully Ravine came up in a conversation with one of his mates, who read the message with a cynical smirk on his face. He referred to it as *"Land-of-Hope-and-Glory-Bullshit,"* and delivered this interpretation:

Dad's mate made this comment: *"Thanks, boys, we sent you out to fight, and you did. We sent you to pull off an impossible job, and you did. You followed orders, you've lost your mates and you're almost done, but we're patting you on the back because you've been good soldier boys."*

I thought Dad's mate summed up the situation pretty well.

All Dad said was: *"Nobody has to say thanks for anything in a war like that. You do your job and that's it. No more, no less. What else could anyone have said?"*

The outcome of the Battle of Gully Ravine: The Allies took the Krithia trenches; they did not take Achi Baba. They never could; they never would. Amen.

JULY 3

We are still on a spell. Things were a bit lively up in the Front Line last night. Very heavy fire on the left and in front of Quinn's Post but pretty quiet on our front.

JULY 4

We took over a small strip of trench to help the 9th Battalion last night, but things are pretty quiet. A very big battle has been raging all day at Cape Helles. We have not heard of any attack, but the Turks may be attacking the Tommies. The Turks opened up a very heavy rifle and machine-gun fire on our front today at 3 o'clock but did not attempt to attack. We were ready for them if they did.

The *"very big battle"* was the Turks counter-attacking the British at Cape Helles; an inevitable move after their Gully Ravine defeat, which had hit them hard. With Krithia temporarily exposed, Achi Baba was now on the list of endangered species. Kemal and von Sanders, the two Ottoman bruiser boys, had no intention of giving the Allies time to pop corks or blow trumpets.

They fired up their Turkish regiments, bundled them into a formidable task force and turned them loose on the northern line of Allied trenches that kept Cape Helles on the safe side of the enemy. The overheated skirmish raged on for two hard days and reached a reckless peak. The Brits, riding a wave of confidence, held the winning cards. Cape Helles was loaded to the hilt with ammunition from supply depots on the Greek islands and the enemy copped salvo after salvo that rocked the ground they were standing on. In no mood for that treatment, the Ottoman masterminds, once again playing the numbers game, pounded the Cape Helles trenches with wave after wave of yelling Turkish soldiers.

But this time the numbers game turned on them and bit deep. The Turkish attack was so relentless that spent bodies were piling up in front of the Allied trenches. When the count nudged thousands, the dismayed Ottomans, reeling from the enormity of the body count, halted the attack. While the smoke-thick air hung over the trenches, and the smell of death began to ripen, the Grapevine reported that the Ottomans called for a truce to bury their dead. Alarmingly, the ailing Aylmer Hunter-Western, still in command at Cape Helles at that point, refused. His officers, aghast at the callousness of the refusal, begged him to reconsider. Again, he refused; reasoning that the dead bodies would have a negative psychological impact on the morale of the attacking Turkish soldiers.

Confirmation of this incident is hard to find, but it came to the boil on the Cove Grapevine. Dad also heard if from Costas, who had picked it up from a French journalist on one of the supply boats.

> THE JOURNALIST: *"What did the Ottomans expect? It's the law of the jungle on Gallipoli. You don't ask for favours and you don't get any. They send their men to certain death and call us inhuman when we won't agree to help bury them."*

Dad said his mates, who'd witnessed their own truce burial in May, seriously questioned the rumour. My father preferred to think it wasn't true but admitted the possibility:

> *"Things were bad. Men weren't thinking like men anymore. It was awful but there was nothing anyone could do about it. Things had gone past that."*

The truce story, still racing along the Grapevine, got this response from one of the commissioned officers at the Cove:

"Whatever happened to valour and gallantry? We used to be human beings with human responsibilities. What in heaven's name is happening to us?"

Whether the burial request was true or not, the Ottoman counter-attack on Cape Helles was temporarily put on hold when von Sanders realised it was futile; even so, he would have been comforted to know that despite the enormity of the body count, Achi Baba, his prized Gallipoli baby, was still safe in its untouchable cradle.

THE PLOT THICKENS: THE CALM BEFORE ANOTHER STORM

JULY 5

We are still in the Firing Line and things are still quiet on our front, but the Turks are easily baited. They just wait for us to send up a star shell and they fire like one thing all night. They fire 100 shots to our one. I think we have the wind up them properly.

JULY 6

Still in the firing line and I was out on patrol last night. Things were quiet, and we crawled right up close to the Turks and could hear them talking, but there were only about 12 of them. They were too close to their own trenches for us to try a fight. They may have set a trap for us, so we stayed out till daylight, came in and had a decent sleep all day.

JULY 7

We got relieved and went into reserve trenches last night but had to stand to nearly all night. They started shelling our trenches and opened up a very heavy rifle fire but did not attack. We spent the day carrying up rations and ammunition from Brigade Headquarters. We would give a lot for some decent food. Bully beef and biscuits and bacon is rough, with bread only once a week and a loaf between four of us.

JULY 8

Went into the firing line again last night. The Jackos were kicking up a lot of row all night and singing out. It is one of their religious festivals and they are supposed to do desperate things this month. They will find a pretty desperate mob over this way if they attack. The only thing will be if they bring up a fresh division to take us on, they will eat us, as I don't think we could ever last out.

JULY 9

We stood to again last night, and we had to sleep with our boots on and all our equipment strapped on. It was hard, but it had to be done. Did not get too much sleep, about two hours best. Last night was all we got. Another thing we found out today was that the Jackos do not eat anything at all during the day, not until after 7 p.m., hence all the hell's delight of a night when they are feasting. If they only have bully beef and biscuits, they can't enjoy it much.

Jackos? Dad's nickname for Turks; the closest he could get to Jackals, which was what the Royal Scots had called them after Gully Ravine. The Big Muslim festival, obviously Ramadan, had the Jackos doing well in the catering department. No doubt their party tucker, piles of it, was coming across from Çanakkale on supply boats.

Dad gripes a bit; who could blame him? Here's the enemy living it up on fancy eats while the Cove trench menus ran to bully beef, stale cheese, and hard biscuits. Festival rules (according to Dad): Food was taboo from sunup to sundown; after that, anything goes.

JULY 10

Have we got to suffer this for a month? The Jackos were having a circus again last night and we had to stand to nearly all night. One thing; they do not do much firing now at night but have been at it all day and we have to be ready for them night and day with all our equipment and boots on. We did not get much sleep last night; only for about three hours and with everything on.

JULY 11

We were out on patrol last night. The Jackos did a lot of firing during the night and were having a fine time. We chased their patrol in and they started up again and were going all night but in case they came back, we just lay flat outside the Front Line till just before daylight and came in. Had a man hit through the thigh just as we were coming in.

JULY 12

There was not much doing last night. The Jackos were pretty quiet but they might be preparing for an attack. We had to be ready for them if they came. There has been another big battle at Achi Baba since daylight and it has been raging all day. The battleships and destroyers have been bombarding since daylight and the rifle fire has been heavy. We have heard it all day and it has not ceased for a minute. It is still raging at 6 o'clock tonight.

Another *"big battle"* at Cape Helles; another stalemate!

Can you imagine how Ian Hamilton must have felt? Seventy-eight days had passed since he pushed the go-button on landings at Cape Helles, and Achi Baba was still firmly in the hands of the enemy, not a bad holdout on the part of the Ottoman heavies. Had Hamilton been a gin and tonic man, *and I don't know whether he was or not*, there would hardly have been enough gin on call to ease his frustration and disappointment.

The state of play in the Dardanelles Campaign on July 12, 1915: Not good for the Allies: Cape Helles was gobbling up supplies of ammunition like an elephant on a peanut binge, and all of it may just as well have been gift-wrapped and sent to the Turks as a festival present.

There were no presents of any kind for the Allies. The kitchens on Lemnos and Imbros were working overtime, but the boys in

Dad's trenches were still hungry. Supply lanes to and from the Greek islands were running hot every hour of every day, sun-up to sundown. Shipments of flour and other items; cheese, water, biscuits, and meat had to come from the Grecian mainland.

Fuel for the Sopwiths was shipped in from Alexandria, or from the French Riviera, Gibraltar, and Great Britain. Medical supplies were topped up non-stop. Nurses, weakened by the dire conditions and the daily death toll, were at their wits end with fatigue and concern. *Seventy-eight days!*

The Ottomans were having their ups-and-downs, but in brighter moments it was the Ramadan Follies and they were a decent chorus line! There were no standing ovations for the Allies. Cape Helles had become a land-locked fortress with its back to the beautiful sea.

Anzac Cove with its trench posts, one beach, and thousands of inmates, was Gallipoli's Devils Island; easy to get into, a miracle to get out of.

Neighbouring hostile Bulgaria sat ready to enter the war at the drop of an Ottoman plea, and there was the Dardanelles fleet in the Aegean Sea; cruisers, battleships, and destroyers, all waiting for the next move, without knowing what the next move would be.

In the sky above, the Sopwith Camel pilots cruised on reconnaissance flights over the action down below; hoping they were not just joy-riding. In the lice-ridden trenches of Anzac Cove, Dad and the lads wondered how they would ever get the blood and grime out of their tunics, boots and hair, and how they could continue to endure the flies, the lice, the dysentery, the appalling conditions, the steaming heat of summer and the stench of death that hung over everything.

The endless longing for home never left them. Australia and New Zealand—beautiful and clean and sweet; pretty towns with pretty people; fresh bread and apple pies and mango trees; smiles and loving arms and cattle dogs asleep on the warm soil of a dead fire. All so far away. And there's Dad; not alone yet all alone; closing his eyes in the trenches and seeing Rockhampton. This he wrote about home on the last pages of his diary:

> *To give anyone a brief description of the Dardanelles and the country is to just take them out to sea and look at it with them: It is just like standing on the bank of the Fitzroy River in Rocky and looking towards the Berseker Ranges. You could hardly tell the difference in the two places.*

He was not hallucinating. He made the same comparisons when he talked about Gallipoli back home, and he made them in his mind on the high hills of Anzac Cove when he wondered if he would ever see the Fitzroy River or the Berseker Ranges again. Seventy-eight days in the godless world of Gallipoli where the angels feared to fly. Seventy-eight days! Still no word of the hoped-for retreat that could have ended it all and saved thousands of lives. Fate turned a blind eye, and with no mercy at all, it would soon be poised to turn another one.

JULY 13

Things were pretty quiet on our front last night. The Jackos were having a good time by the sound of them. We heard today about the attack at Achi Baba which was still going on all night last night. It was not taken, and the Tommies lost very heavily. They reached it twice but could not hold it. If they could only take it, it would be good for us here. So far, it's the same as usual with us. We had to stand by all night at the ready.

Same as usual: Same-old, same-old; same-old tries; same-old knockbacks. Frustration setting in: Generals, Major-Generals, Lieutenant Colonels, and commissioned officers gazing at each other in confusion. An all-night attack on Achi Baba; another game try that got nowhere. Dad and his trench mates were standing to in full battle dress, just in case they were needed to add a bit of clout, all the while waiting and hoping for just one breath of good news, while the Jackos partied and got ready to pelt the Cove with a few more star shells and sneaky salvos from a sniper. A minor change was on the way for Dad; he didn't know it yet, but it was in the wind.

JULY 14

We were out on patrol last night, but the Turks were out in force and drove us back. We did not go out anymore and things went quiet and have stayed that way all day.

JULY 15

I was moved into the 2nd Brigade Machine Gun section today and got one sniper: Will not have to go out on any more patrols now. I have been I/C of the guns all day. Things have been quiet. We got orders not to open up our machine guns until the Turks attack.

The change he didn't want! He was not a machine gunner, he didn't want to be one and he said so; killing was bad enough with a rifle; with a machine gun, it was worse. He got the post because he was a sergeant and they said he'd been lucky. The one bright note: *no more patrols!*

JULY 16

Things were quiet again last night on our front but heavy fire at Courtney's Ridge. We did not get much rest last night, but we had a few hours' sleep early this morning beside our guns. All our equipment is ready.

JULY 17

Things quiet on our front again last night. Everything has gone quiet everywhere and has been like that all day. A Taube flew over us this afternoon but the guns on the battleship drove it away. It did no damage. We stood to almost all night. If they are going to attack, I wish they would. We are just about fed up with all of this.

"*Just about fed up with all this,*" says Dad. He and the lads have their hats in the ring for a Jacko attack that didn't happen. Apparently, the silence was too much. Unless the air was being ripped to bits by gunfire and star shells, things didn't feel right. Gallipoli's killing field reputation was in danger of being upstaged by the sounds of silence! *It didn't last.*

JULY 18

The Turks did a good deal of firing on our Front Line, last night and drove our patrol in. We lost a few more men. The 9th Battalion Patrol captured the Turkish Patrol and brought them in. They were 12 men and one German officer.

JULY 19

Things about the same as last night: Not too much doing but we had to stand to again all night in case the Turks attacked.

JULY 20

We shifted one of our machine guns into a better position last night, but things have been quiet on all fronts. There was a lot of shelling going on at daylight, but 8 battleships came on the scene and opened up on them and they have kept quiet all day.

JULY 21

Things quiet all night and all day. Nothing doing anywhere but we had to stand to again all night.

JULY 22

Things still quiet along our front but lively up on the left where the New Zealanders are. We have not fired a shot with our machine guns since I came over to them but have had to stand to as we are still expecting the Turks every night. We have not had our boots off for 14 days, and only getting about 2 hours sleep a night and sometimes a few hours during the day.

JULY 23

Still in the firing line: Things were lively last night on our front. The Jackos started shelling us at about 7 p.m. and kept it up till about 9 p.m. Things stayed lively all night as they kept up a heavy rifle and machine-gun fire. Our patrol could not go out, but things have been quiet since morning.

JULY 24

A Gurkha Mountain Battery came up and took up a position just behind our lines last night. They were shelling the Turks all night and have been on them all day. They have kept them quiet and there has not been much fire from them at all.

JULY 25

We were relieved last night and came out of the trenches. We had a good night's sleep and had our boots off and our heavy equipment off for the first time in sixteen days and what a relief it was. We went down to the beach and had a swim today and the water was lovely.

The water was lovely! You bet it was. At the end of the rickety pier, the water was close to 15 feet deep, perfect for diving but always dangerous. Turkish snipers never missed a chance to pick off men in the water. Apart from relief, the seawater inhibited the lice and fleas that infested the trenches and grimy uniforms worn for days on end. Soaking garments in the saltwater gave temporary relief but when insect infestations were full bore, the only remedy was to soak clothes and blankets with insecticide. Imagine what that did to human skin.

There is a touching story of one soldier who befriended a little dog that had somehow ventured onto the Peninsula. At the Cove, it went everywhere with him and he was told he could keep it despite the no-dog rule. The soldier and his pet were swimming one day when Beachy Bill opened fire and the little pooch caught a bullet. The sadness of the scene was lightened for a few precious moments when that little dog was given a special farewell and a soldier's funeral. Life doesn't have to be big to be beautiful. The heartbroken soldier took a breath, stiffened his upper lip, and soldiered on.

JULY 26

Still out of the firing line and we are having a rest. We had some stew today and got tea twice. Things have been lively today with plenty of shell fire and a lot of the Gurkha Regiment killed and wounded. The Turks got right onto them with shell fire.

JULY 27

While I was down on the beach today. I saw Tom Stafford; he is with the 2nd Light Horse Field Ambulance and we had a good talk about old times in Barcaldine. We both wish we were back there again. We are still out of the Firing Line and have been making the most of the day. That is the spell we needed but we had to get out the pick and shovel to dig more trenches and carry more ammunition up the hill.

After twelve weeks, my father is tired. Lonelier, too. Twelve weeks are not an eternity; days can fly by in a flash but not if you're wishing and hoping to be somewhere else. He's standing for hours in his heavy dirty boots. He's digging deep into the dirt of Gallipoli with a pick and shovel. He's lugging heavy ammunition up to the trenches, boxes of bullets and shells that will kill more men than he will ever meet in his lifetime.

In all of this, his heaven is Barcaldine, the little town in the faraway Utopia of Queensland, his jackaroo stamping ground. He yarns about it to Tom Stafford, one of his old mates, a field ambulance man exposed to the pain and suffering of hundreds of wounded men.

Both of them had been on Gallipoli since early May. Both had been through the hell of it, seen the worst of it, felt the desperation of it. They were not alone. By now, it would have been clear to Boss Birdwood and his team of commissioned officers, that the fighting men at Anzac Cove had come close to the end of their endurance.

My father faced every day as it came. The longer he survived the more he wondered how much more time he had left. When would his luck run out? But when you'd cheated death as often as he had, every day was another run on the board. Another dawn, another day, another sundown. The fighting was "awful," he said;

but almost as bad was the isolation and uncertainty of who was winning, and worse, how it would end; every day filled with the fear of capture; having to exist in a Turkish prison or dying with no one to care.

On the battlefronts of the Middle East and the Western Front, an unavoidable impasse had set in. Every move The Allies made to attack the Dardanelles forts was checked by Ottoman resistance.

In London, Georgie's Boys were getting nowhere. On Gallipoli, thousands of fighting men lived in limbo; the military and bureaucratic manoeuvring that controlled their lives was past understanding. North of the Black Sea the Russians waited anxiously for the promised sea lane, and on the fields of Flanders, the senseless combat went on and on. Chaos reigned, while on the other side of the Atlantic Ocean, the New World, not yet part of the conflict, watched and waited while the rest of the world watched them.

So went The Great War; the monstrous prowling tiger lost in a baffling maze of its own making; and in the end, nothing more than a blood-soaked lesson in *"How Not to Give In."*

OUT OF THE TERRIBLE DARKNESS: A NEW HOPE

JULY 28

We are out digging roads and it is hard work, just as dangerous as in the Firing Line. There is so much shell fire coming this way that the working parties are losing a lot of men.

JULY 29

We are still digging roads all day but no night work. We rested till 9 o'clock last night and then we slept. We stood to at half-past three this morning.

JULY 30

Had a rest till daylight and went back into the Firing Line again but not much doing on our front. Very heavy fire on the Tommie's front and star shells going up all night but we were quiet until daylight.

JULY 31

We had a very lively night last night. The Turks opened up on us at midnight and kept it up till daybreak and then it died away. Things have been quiet all day.

AUGUST 1

The Turks were shelling us last night and we lost more men, but the New Zealanders and the 4th Infantry Brigade were attacked. Somehow, they held their line and drove the Turks off.

AUGUST 2

Very heavy fire on our front last night and they shelled us all day. We were sure they would attack but they did not.

AUGUST 3

A lot of new artillery was landed last night. The Tommies were pulling their guns up all night. Everything is shifted in at night, so it cannot be seen during the day. We have found out what we were making the roads for.

Much speculation! A happening on the way!

Tommies and heavy guns. Secret roads on the seaside ridges of Anzac Cove. Artillery being landed at night. The messages were clear: *A new offensive in the wind; what else?*

The men knew no more than that on Tuesday, August 3, 1915, but maybe this was the positive move they had all been waiting for. The guessing game was on, fingers crossed. The Cove was abuzz with curiosity. And optimism! *Positive movement in London at long last?*

After four months of blistering retaliation from the defending Ottoman army, a firm decision to turn the battle around had finally been tabled. Lloyd George's mindset was unswerving: He'd had enough of Gallipoli. He wanted the Ottoman Empire on its knees, and he pushed the Dardanelles Committee into action. The result was big, and it was decisive.

The Ottoman forts had to be taken, the mines in the narrows had to be blown sky high and the guns of Çanakkale with them! Who did the Turks think they were? Who did they think they were dealing with?

With the narrows undefended and the on-shore guns silenced, Churchill was on stand-by to steam his armada up the Dardanelles through the Sea of Marmara to take possession of Constantinople at last!

No argument this time. No excuses. *It was on the cards, a winning hand!*

After long days of studying photographs taken by Sopwith reconnaissance pilots, Lloyd George's decision, backed by the Dardanelles Committee, was set in strategic cement. A new Gallipoli Front Line was to be established to facilitate a combined offensive that would shatter Turkish resistance once and for all. The new line would begin at Gaba Tepe, curve north-west past Anzac Cove and Lone Pine, then continue on to Hill 971. It would run past the Turkish outposts of Chunuk Bair and Tekke Tepe right up to Ejelmer Bay, miles away on the mid-northern shore of the Peninsula. Contained within the eastern sweep of the new line was the wide virgin beach of Suvla Bay, a few miles north of the Cove, the chosen spot for the beginning of the end of the Gallipoli stalemate. Both Anzac Cove and Suvla Bay were to be armed to the teeth and readied for the challenge.

Lloyd George was not mucking about, not this time. His latest juggernaut would be powered by twenty-thousand British troops, the A-List of the Empire. Upon landing at Suvla Bay they were to establish a base, move south-west to meet with battle-savvy soldiers moving north from Anzac Cove. The combined force would then move south down the wild Gallipoli terrain to meet with the British regiments coming up from Cape Helles to form a mighty push due west to take out the guns on the eastern shores of the Dardanelles, blow up the mines in the narrows, put paid to the Çanakkale fortress on the western shore of the strategic waterway, and wipe the arrogant smiles off the faces of Liman von Sanders, Mustafa Kemal, and the Ottoman army.

The invincible might of the British Empire; triumph at last!

Lloyd George, driven on by furious energy, was determined. No more blunders. No more duds. He had the Ottoman Empire in his sights, and he was hot to trot. This was it! Finally! *Do-or-die!* He had decided to make his move, and move he did!

Heavy guns and ammunition had already been landed and trundled at midnight along the cliff-top roads at Anzac Cove. Fresh regiments of British troops were assembling in the Greek islands, with their eyes on Suvla Bay, the chosen spot for the surprise attack, *the secret jack in the box!*

But behind the closed doors of the military, the ever-present, ever-exasperated critics of the Dardanelles Campaign shook their heads: *Was this more madness?*

They had a point: Suvla Bay, located on the eastern shore of the widest part of the Peninsula, was at least twelve miles away from the Dardanelles forts over hostile land that dipped and dived all over the place; awkward to transverse and peppered with well-defended Turkish outposts.

One military brain gazed at the map and said: *"How do they think they'll pull this attack off? Do*

> *they know what an obstacle course that unruly terrain is? How can they hope to keep the regiments together? It's the most ridiculous offensive of this entirely ridiculous campaign. Didn't they study the reconnaissance photography? Lloyd George must be out of his mind!"*

If so, nobody was telling him. On the drawing board, the plan wore the pen-and-ink glow of success, but like so many Gallipoli blunders, this one was sabotaged by an amazingly stupid mistake. Its name was Lieutenant-General Sir Frederick Stopford, chosen for the task of commanding the offensive, despite a strident vote of disapproval from the war-weary Sir Ian Hamilton, who argued that Stopford, then aged 61, was too old for the assignment.

To make matters worse it was later divulged that Stopford was handed the tough job, not on laurels or experience, but because he was next in senior line! And so it appears that David Lloyd George's titanic plan for the wipe-out of the Ottoman Empire rested on the declining abilities of a high-end soldier whose sharpness had been blunted by time.

But blithely assigning Ian Hamilton's objections to the waste paper basket, The Dardanelles Committee green-lighted the plan and toasted the Union Jack, safe in the assumption that the Ottomans would be taken by surprise.

Again? Didn't anyone do their homework?

Activating his *little grey cells*, the perceptive German General, Otto Limon von Sanders, realising the British Empire was on the ropes in the Dardanelles, knew that the powers in London would never tolerate such a comedown for too long. Well aware that any further moves to turn the war around would have to come from the Aegean Sea, he despatched a team of eagle-eyed scouts to the Greek islands to watch for any unusual movements.

When his scouts reported a continuing build-up of British troops on Greek soil, von Sanders sensed an imminent attack on Gallipoli, and he didn't have to be an Oxford Professor to guess where it would happen.

Suvla Bay had lights all over it!

It was presently unoccupied, easily accessible from the Aegean Sea, close to Anzac Cove, far enough away from Cape Helles to be safe from the major Turkish regiments at Krithia and Achi Baba, and only short miles away from the established trenches of the Allies at Anzac Cove on the eastern seaboard.

Closely north-west of Anzac Cove sat The Nek, a narrow passage in the hills that afforded entry to the near-southern high ground of Suvla Bay. The eagle eyes of von Sanders immediately registered its importance. Due west of The Nek, and overlooking it, was the high grassy knoll of Baby 700, an almost too perfect threat to any troop movement through The Nek if it could be filled with Turkish guns, which is exactly what Otto von Sanders did. He also despatched three divisions of soldiers, fifteen thousand in all, to cover the crescent-shaped curve of Suvla Bay from three vantage points directly above the beach. They were Kiretch Tepe, overlooking the northern point of the Suvla Bay crescent; Hill 10, centre-north of it; and Lala Baba, centre-south of it. Behind Lala Baba was a wide salt-lake. Overlooking the lake's western edge was Chocolate Hill, also fortified by von Sanders. Although the Brits were not aware of it, von Sanders had made Suvla Bay as vulnerable as a sitting duck. Still the perfectionist, he was not finished.

In case he'd missed his guess on the Suvla Bay location, he sent another three divisions to Bulair, overlooking the Gulf of Saros 30 miles to the north, his alternative guess for the landing, even though he reasoned that it was too far away to be a possibility. But the wily von Sanders was taking no chances: He wasn't sure of the exact size of the attacking Allied force, but he knew after examining reports from his scouts that it wasn't small.

He also knew something the Brits were all too vague about. The waters off Suvla Bay were networked with sandy shoals of uneven depth that would not be easy to navigate, particularly for soldiers loaded down with heavy ammunition. As such, they would be easy targets if they were forced to stumble around on shaky footing with their boots filled with sand and seawater. Still, the arithmetic was hardly in Otto's favour: fifteen thousand against twenty thousand may not have seemed like a winning wager, but he was willing to take the punt.

The British were so full of confidence that Turkish scouts suspiciously nosing around on the Greek islands had failed to come to their notice. The wily Otto knew Gallipoli; he knew a landing at Suvla Bay would be no pushover, and he guessed that the Brits were desperate enough to be over-confident. While he cooled his heels, watching and waiting for the inevitable, the scene was being set for Lloyd George's brazen attempt to turn the tides of war into waves of victory.

The top-secret invasion was scheduled to begin under cover of darkness at 10 p.m. on the night of August 6. The twenty thousand-strong British task force was expected to be in possession of Suvla Bay by dawn on August 7.

According to reliable accounts, three major Allied offensives were timed to begin on August 6 to divert the enemy's attention from the eastern seaboard of the Gallipoli Peninsula and the Suvla Bay target.

The First: A Cape Helles-British attack on Krithia Vineyard south-south-west of Anzac Cove. *The Second*: an ANZAC attack on the Turkish held trenches at Lone Pine, south-west of the Cove. *The Third:* an ANZAC advance to take Baby 700, just west of The Nek.

Lloyd George had approved the convoluted strategy that had clearly taken hours of plotting and planning, even more hours of consultation, briefing and consolidating. Here are the three diverting offensives in further detail:

One: The two-pronged British attack on Krithia Vineyard from Cape Helles, designed to implement Hamilton's original plan to take Achi Baba prior to a northern advance to join the western bound British regiments after they landed at Suvla Bay.

Two: The ANZACs were to attack Lone Pine, breakthrough to join a northern British push from Cape Helles, then meet up with the newly landed British regiments west of Suvla Bay. The merged force would then move across the Peninsula to the new Front Line, and from there to the Ottoman gun batteries on the western seaboard of the Peninsula.

Three: A combined force of Light Horse artillery made up of the 8th and 10th regiments from Victoria and Western Australia, were to charge through The Nek to attack the Turkish-held Baby 700 to prevent any hampering of the British advance from Suvla Bay. This offensive was to be backed by Churchill's battleships scheduled to begin shelling Baby 700 twenty minutes before the Light Horse regiments were timed to move. Further assistance here was to come from a New Zealand regiment primed to take the Turkish-held hill of Chunuk Bair, over a mile away to the north-west, before moving to assist the Light Horse Regiments at The Nek.

On paper, the strategy was perfectly planed and imposing. How could it go wrong?

AUGUST 4

The 11th Battalion attacked and took the Tasmania Post just north of us three days ago. We kept up heavy cover fire all night on the Turkish front. Last night we heard that our colonel had been killed. He was shot through the head and died right away. We also lost three more men.

The capture of the Turkish-held Tasmania Post by the 11th Battalion after an earlier failure five days before, strengthened the Suvla Bay strategy by clearing the way for the planned Victorian and Western Australian move on The Nek.

The dead colonel was Hubert Jennings Imbrie Harris, aged 44, who joined the 5th Light Horse on October 28, 1914. He had been shot in one of the earlier attacks on the Tasmania Post on Saturday, July 31. He was succeeded by Brigadier General Lachlan Wilson, who fought in the Boer War. Lachlan Wilson joined the regiment in September 1914 and survived Gallipoli. Colonel Harris was admired, trusted and knowledgeable. His death was a major blow to his men; gone when they needed him most.

AUGUST 5

Things have been lively all day all along our front. Very heavy fire all night and all day, it has not stopped.

AUGUST 6

We got reinforcements last night and at daylight this morning the Turks attacked the 11th Battalion and drove them out of Tasmania Post but the 11th took it back with bayonets and drove the Turks out. We held them off with machine-gun fire as they were returning for a counter-attack. Up to 100 can be seen lying between the trenches. It was them or us.

HOW THE MIGHTY FELL:
SUVLA BAY: DO OR DIE

ON THE AFTERNOON OF AUGUST 6, the Suvla Bay landing was set in place and ready to go as planned. The combined offensive was fully dependent on perfect timing and the success of every one of its components. Confidence ruled. By nightfall, the massive sea-bound invasion force was ready to be ferried to the shore, not in the clumsy boats that carried the ANZACs, but in cunningly-conceived self-propelled landing craft known as "Beetles" swishing silently through the water under cover of darkness.

Meanwhile, unknown to the Brits, the Turks were keeping their beady eyes on Anzac Cove, and thanks to the sharp mind of Otto von Sanders, well-armed Ottoman soldiers lurked at the ready in fortified outposts all over the mid-eastern hills of the Peninsula.

At the same time, the men in Dad's regiment at Anzac Cove, seasoned by weeks of star shells, snipers, and sleepless nights, fully charged on adrenalin, had no intention of letting the enemy get away with anything preventable. They had found their second wind. They were not naïve enough to expect a barroom brawl, but at last something positive was brewing; it was in the air.

> DAD: *"We could feel it; it was all over the place. For the first time in weeks, we had a reason to be bright-eyed about something and we were all ready for whatever it was."*

And "whatever it was" was beginning to happen.

The pieces of the mighty Suvla Bay jigsaw puzzle were coming together.

At Anzac Cove, Dad's lads, primed by their morning win, were alert, edgy and waiting for more.

At Cape Helles, the battle-honed Tommies, under the command of Aylmer-Hunter's experienced replacement, General Street, had been well-briefed on their attack on Krithia Vineyard, and they were gearing up.

At the same time, the Light Horse Regiments were gathering at the entrance of The Nek as the sun went down.

Miles further north, the New Zealanders were grouping to take Chunuk Bair from the Turks, before moving to assist in the attack on The Nek and Baby 700.

Out in the Aegean Sea, Churchill's battleships sat under a starry sky; their guns trained on the eastern landscape of Gallipoli, while the whispering Beetles were set to be loaded and launched from their destroyer escorts. Everything was going to plan; everything was looking good.

But under the same starry skies, Ottoman soldiers, alerted by the forward planning of Otto von Sanders, quietly waited to defend their home ground, fully keyed to the fact that somewhere out yonder in the Aegean Sea thousands of enemy troops were expecting to surprise them with an overwhelming force of arms.

In the still of the night, the hand of Fate paused; then at 10 p.m. on Friday, August 6, 1915, it moved to accomplish its purpose. Under cover of darkness, the silent Beetles, loaded with Allied fighting men hit the starlit sea and silently glided towards the beach at Suvla Bay.

Yet another unforgettable Gallipoli weekend was underway.

On paper, the British Master Plan that had looked so big, bold, and workable, registered an unexpected turn. Once again, a fickle twist turned the Suvla Bay jack-in-the-box into a monstrous mess that sent minds into a spin.

In order, not necessarily of preference, here's how the hands of Fate tore the pages of Lloyd George's well-laid plan to shreds:

In an almost perfect replay of the first Anzac assault on Anzac Cove, the ships that launched the first wave of Beetles were too far away from the shore, and the distance was misjudged. Men leaped out of the landing craft into deep water and did their best to flounder through the treacherous sandy shoals to the shore, exactly as von Sanders had predicted. While that was happening, the moon rose, exposing the attacking regiments to Turkish snipers positioned on Lala Baba and Hill 10 just above the beach. Caught in the hail of bullets were several of the task force's commanding officers. With the leaders of the pack diminished in number, hundreds of fighting men deprived of orders and direction stumbled in lost confusion to the beach.

> "We were told to take Hill 10," one survivor said,
> "but we didn't know where Hill 10 was."

The Turkish snipers knew. They were sitting in it.

So where was the illustrious Lieutenant-General Sir Frederick Stopford, the man in charge of the operation? Unlike Boss Birdwood, who had personally guided the ANZACs through the jumble of the Anzac Cove landing, the Lieutenant-General was asleep on board the sloop *HMS Jonquil*, way out there in the Aegean Sea. He was awakened at 4 a.m. when it was suggested by a commanding officer that it might be wise to find out what was going on.

The charge on The Nek was another mind-numbing miscalculation. Early on the morning of June 7, the guns on Churchill's battleships, due to shell Baby 700 twenty minutes before the 8th and 10th Light Horse attack on The Nek was timed to start, ceased firing too soon, giving the Turks on Baby 700 time to recover and train their guns on the enemy. Wave after wave of men, the flower of Victorian and West Australian manhood, charged into a firestorm of Turkish bullets and were cut down as they ran. Futile attempts to halt the charge added to the confusion. Finally, after the third wave of 150 men was wiped out to a man, Lt Colonel Brazier, commander of the West Australians, managed to call the attack off—all too late.

Worse still, the New Zealand division directed to assist The Light Horsemen failed to take Chunuk Bair until the following day and were dealt out of the battle. If they'd been successful at Chunuk Bair and able to attack Baby 700 from the rear, they may have saved the Light Horsemen. It didn't happen.

The abysmal massacre of The Nek has gone down in history as one of the most tragic blunders of the dodgy campaign.

Gallipoli wept, and the world weeps to this day.

At Krithia Vineyard, the Turks successfully held off the Tommies, and another piece of the plan fell apart. But it wasn't over yet . . .

AUGUST 7

Things were lively last night and a lot of fire. Today our batteries opened up a very heavy fire on the Turkish trenches and at half-past five, the first Australian Infantry Brigade took Lone Pine after very severe fighting that began yesterday afternoon at sunset. We could see the battle quite plainly and there were very heavy losses, many hundreds can be seen lying dead beside the trenches in No Man's Land. It's worse than awful. We couldn't do anything, and the battle continued all night.

Lone Pine was another story altogether: a festival of horrors!

At 5:30 p.m. on the afternoon of August 6, 1915, after a day of hard fighting, a total of four thousand ANZACs from the 1st, 2nd and 3rd Brigades circled the craggy hills behind the Turkish trenches at Lone Pine and steeled themselves to cross the Daisy Patch to attack from the west, forcing the Turks to fire into the setting sun. When the whistle blew, men jumped parapets to thunder across the 100-yard gap separating the battle lines, to join the yelling scramble for the target. Ripping their uniforms to ribbons, the men negotiated the barbed wire barriers and leaped, dived, or stumbled into the enemy trenches. As the screams of the wounded and dying split the air and rose above the relentless cacophony of gunfire and the terrifying clash of bayonets, they fought with all the strength they could pull from their firm young bodies, while their minds, all but frozen by the savagery of the battle, drove them on, many to a terrible death on the bloody bayonets of the doomed and torn enemy.

Once in charge of the Turkish trenches, they stood on, or lay over, or pushed aside the bodies of the dead to breathe into their parched lungs the stinking rancid air of the costly ANZAC victory, forever unable to come to grips with what they'd been through.

In my father's trenches, two miles away in the fading light of the setting sun, Dad and his mates watched in mute disbelief as the sights and screams of the battle shredded their senses. Too stunned to move; too appalled to weep, and too shocked to believe what they were seeing, they looked to heaven and prayed for a miracle to shut out the pain and despair of the wounded and dying splattered all over The Daisy Patch and the bloodied trenches of Lone Pine. Nobody said a word.

My Dad's heart broke that day; he put it back together because he needed it to keep him going, but he lost some of the pieces, and I don't think he ever found them.

He told me about Lone Pine one night after we'd been at an Anzac Day service not long after the Second World War ended. He was in one of his quiet moods, sitting in the soft light on the veranda of our house. He'd been there for ages not saying anything, so I went out to ask him what was wrong. He told me in detail of what he'd seen at Lone Pine all those years before. It was the only time I saw him take a stiff drink and the only time I saw him break down.

The official death tally at Lone Pine is less than my father's but it is still shattering. Stories of that battle have been told and retold hundreds of times, and in greater gore and detail. Dad doesn't say much in his diary. He doesn't have to. Despite all that had gone wrong, the plan to establish a new Allied Front Line on the Gallipoli Peninsula was still up front with the heavies.

When will they never learn?

AUGUST 8

The battle along our front is still raging. Every brigade is in it and there has been a new landing at Suvla Bay. Two British divisions landed, and the place is a living hell. We have advanced our line from one end to the other, we have just heard the 8th Light Horse has been wiped right out and the wounded are going out to the hospital ships in hundreds all day. Small boats towing lighters all day with wounded men. We advanced our line last night with hardly any loss. The battle is still raging harder than ever. Tonight, every gun on our front is barking and the battleships at Suvla Bay are firing too. Streams of wounded men are going out to sea and there are dead men everywhere. The 1st Infantry Division lost over 3,000 men taking Lone Pine.

AUGUST 9

We had orders to pack up our guns last night and go up to reinforce the 4th Australian Infantry Brigade near Hill 971 as nearly all their machine gunners were wiped out. We started out at 9 o'clock and reached them at half-past ten. The battle was raging when we got there. We got into action right away. The sight going up was awful; dead and wounded everywhere. The Brigade had two tries to take it during the night but could not. They got into it this morning and the Turks came in thousands to drive them off. We fired at them, but they still came on. We managed to hold them at their old line, but the battle is raging harder than ever now.

Hill 971 was well over 3 miles north-west of the Anzac Cove trenches. To get there, the 90-minute manoeuvre would have taken my father's regiment past the slaughter field of The Nek, and the New Zealanders holding out at Chunuk Bair. The Turks had written off the Allied plans for Suvla Bay, but they had lost heavy ground at Lone Pine. Temporarily on the back foot, they did their best to save Hill 971 but lost it after Dad's regiment added clout to the 4th Brigade's move to take it over and hold it.

AUGUST 10

The battle is still raging. We got a Gurkha Brigade last night to reinforce us and the Turks have been attacking us all night. We have had no water since we came here and have been fighting all the time. The New Zealanders on our left took a Turkish line today. The battle is still going very heavy at Suvla Bay. The Gurkhas have been cut up badly today. They came right back, and the 4th Brigade stopped the Turks again.

AUGUST 11

The battle is still raging all along our front and we are just holding on waiting for the Tommies to join us, but I think the Suvla Bay landing is a failure as they have not made any advance and we cannot hold out much longer if they don't soon come up on our left flank. The Turks made two desperate attacks to try and shift us today, but they failed. We opened fire on them all afternoon with our machine guns and the wounded are everywhere. It is awful to see.

AUGUST 12

We came back to our old Front Line last night. We could not hold out any longer at Hill 971 as the Suvla Bay landing was a failure. The Tommies have dug in there and our advance was no good because they could not get through to join us. The 4th Infantry Brigade and us have been three days

> *without any water but we got a little this morning. After all we did at Hill 971 nothing was any good because the Suvla Bay landing was a disaster.*

The blame rocketed right to the top then plopped down to land at the feet of the sixty-one-year-old Sir Frederick Stopford, whose performance was leniently described as "appalling." Ian Hamilton had been against the appointment from the beginning—the debacle of Suvla Bay confirmed that opinion; *all too late*. Stopford's critics in the military had plenty of verbal ammunition. They let fly and the barbs came thick and fast— among them were accusations that the man had failed in the correct briefing of his officers; allowing them to be despatched in the dark with little understanding of what they were supposed to be doing.

It got worse: voices were raised in disbelief when it was announced that while the Beetles were headed for disaster in the shoals of Suvla Bay, the sixty-one-year-old Stopford was peacefully snoozing in the comfort of his bunk at sea.

The uproar was so boisterous that everyone forgot who the real culprits were. There is no record of anyone throwing darts at David Lloyd George and the Dardanelles Commission in London. Ian Hamilton, tired and exhausted, shouldered the disgrace. Unfair as that seems, Hamilton was Stopford's superior officer and severest critic, and he had failed to keep the old warrior toeing the line. It was a beaten Hamilton who expressed his dismay as follows:

> *"My heart has grown tough amidst the struggles of the Peninsula, but the misery of this scene well-nigh broke it. Words are of no use".*

Still struggling to cope, Ian Hamilton was finally relieved of his command on October 15, a mental casualty of the war that had finally beaten him. The conflict he believed in, and had so wanted to win, had become an unmitigated failure. His fate was a *fait accompli* in the considered opinion of the earnest Australian correspondent, 29-year-old Richard Murdoch, father of publishing tycoon Rupert Murdoch. Driven to right the abysmal wrongs of the Dardanelles Campaign as he saw them, Richard Murdoch sat down in the office of the Australian High Commissioner in London on Thursday, September 23, 1915, and dictated a letter to be forwarded to the Australian Prime Minister, Andrew Fisher. In it, he referred to the censorship complaints made by Ellis Ashmead-Bartlett and added his own interpretation of how the Gallipoli War had been so outrageously allowed to run off the rails. He pointed his sternest finger at Ian Hamilton and had little regard for the strategic talents of Dad's Boss, William Birdwood.

So powerful were Murdoch's words, keenly adorned by journalistic flourish, that they not only registered with Andrew Fisher but also with prominent members of The Dardanelles Committee, who saw the letter as their saving grace: *Don't blame us, blame Ian Hamilton.*

And they did. *Cheap!* Richard Murdoch's words were widely believed to have been the wordy bullets that took down Ian Hamilton. It happened three weeks and one day after Murdoch dictated his incriminating letter.

In love and war, you play for keeps.

As some sort of creative memorial to the disgrace of Suvla Bay, as well as a poke in the eye for the Brits, Aussie music man Eric Bogle wrote a song called "*And the Band Played Waltzing Matilda*" and recorded it in 1971. The opening verse goes like this:

> *And how well I remember that terrible day*
> *How our blood stained the sand and the water*
> *And of how in that hell that they called Suvla Bay*
> *We were butchered like lambs at the slaughter*
> *Johnny Turk, he was ready, he primed himself well*
> *He rained us with bullets, and he showered us with shell*
> *And in five minutes flat he'd blown us all to hell*
> *Nearly blew us back home to Australia*

Lovely florid stuff. Spot on if you're into melodrama but not if you're into facts. There were no Aussies in the sand and waters of Suvla Bay on that terrible day. Bogle's colourful lyrics present an incorrect word picture that clouds the courageous ANZAC image. Still, the song's strong anti-war feeling came across loud and clear. It was a big hit, also recorded by Joan Baez and the Clancy Brothers. Even though it shines a false light on the facts of Suvla Bay as far as the ANZACs are concerned, it is still performed at various Anzac Day functions. Its strongest fans are those who claim that the celebration of the day in Australia glorifies war. They should study the Gallipoli history books more closely.

So should Eric Bogle.

Another colourful anti-Brit rumour took flight when it was reported that while the ANZACs were being mowed down at Lone Pine and The Nek, British officers were drinking tea on the beaches of Suvla Bay.

Hardly likely; who brewed the tea and where did it come from? In truth, there were too few officers on the beaches of Suvla Bay; one of the reasons why the landing was a misfire. Most of the Brit officers were gunned down in the moonlight as they negotiated the treacherous shoals in the approaches to the beach. The drinking tea story got an airing in Peter Weir's acclaimed Aussie movie, *Gallipoli*, starring a young and spunky Mel Gibson and released in 1981. The tea-drinking reference was another cheap shot that didn't deserve to be aired but it scored an ironic giggle; of course.

It is also dodgy and unfair to both the Brits and the ANZACs, but it still provides ammunition for loudmouthed activists who rail against the celebration of Anzac Day.

Artistic licence covers many aberrations. The film was a huge hit, both here and abroad, the most financially successful Australian movie of its time. It shot the mega-talented Gibson straight through the doors of Hollywood.

In truth, the film's reference to Brit tea drinking is an unfortunate moment that removes some of the bloom from David Williamson's script, and from Peter Weir's heartfelt direction. And that is one unfortunate shame.

Specifically, in light of the fact that although there are rumours of negative ANZAC attitude towards the British on Gallipoli, I can't find evidence of it in my father's diary, and he never mentioned it at home. He and his men had genuine respect for the British officers and men with whom they came in contact. The term "*Tommies*" says a lot; a nickname my father used all the time. He rejected the label "*Whingeing Poms.*"

Dad could never be called "politically correct" but I never heard him use that term to describe a Brit on Gallipoli.

AUGUST 13

When we came back to join our regiment again last night, we heard there were 9,000 wounded since the Suvla Bay landing. They passed through our Dressing Station in the last three days. Every Australian Brigade has been in the battle and we have lost heavily. We heard that the 2nd

Australian Division is on the way from Egypt. If they don't soon arrive, we will not be able to hold Gallipoli any longer. Things were very lively, heavy fire all day. The Turks may attack our line any time. When and if they do, they will get through as we have no support line. Half the regiment is in supports at Lone Pine. Our lines are very thin everywhere.

AUGUST 14

Things quietened down a little last night. Both sides have had enough. Two fresh divisions of Tommies landed here with us, and have gone up to reinforce the New Zealanders, the 4th Australian Infantry Brigade and the 2nd Australian Infantry Brigade. The 1st Australian Infantry Brigade has only 900 men left out of 4,600 after the battle of Lone Pine. The 8th Light Horse Regiment has been wiped out and the 9th and 10th Light Horse Regiments have only a few men left. The 4th Infantry Brigade has only 700 men left out of 4,000. This battle has cost us dearly.

My father is referring to the ANZAC losses incurred at The Nek, Baby 700, Hill 971, and Lone Pine. The wave of optimism that had washed over Anzac Cove in the early days of August had rolled away. In its wake came the shattering thunderbolt of Suvla Bay, the cold-blooded debacle of The Nek and the inhuman tragedy of Lone Pine. Dad and his mates were all but done in; existing on flagging energy; but only just.

AUGUST 15

Things have been quiet all night and all day. We heard that the Southland with the 21st Battalion on board was torpedoed last night near Lemnos island and was towed in without any loss of life. The long talked about 2nd Division is coming from Egypt at last and not before time.

Another fresh division of Tommies landed last night with a lot of artillery and have gone up to the left with the New Zealanders. Things were lively last night but have been quiet all day. They don't seem to think our line wants any help, we can get on the best we can, but I suppose they are wanted on the left more than they are here.

AUGUST 16

A brigade of Indians landed last night and relieved us this morning at daylight. We have come right back from the line and have made dugouts on the side of a hill. All the Australians look a sorry lot after what we have been through this last week, it has been worse than awful.

DAD'S LAST GASP:
THE BEGINNING OF THE END

THESE ARE TIRED ENTRIES. DAD'S losing it. His cool is gone. He's spent. His mates are spent, it's obvious in his diary entries. The rot has set in, and a don't-care attitude has taken over. There's nothing anyone can do. The heaviness of the battles is weighing everyone down. Dad's casualty figures don't tally with official lists. If his numbers came via the Cove Grapevine, they could have been exaggerated, but it's possible that censorship trimmed them back. How anyone was still able to function on Gallipoli defies belief. Life had become a nothing. Powerful Ottoman resistance had wiped out all hope for the establishment of the proposed new Allied Front Line. It was a lost dream, even so, reinforcements were arriving all the time. In the minds of the High Command, the Dardanelles Campaign was still on the A-List, while hopes for victory were evaporating into the weakening heat of the dying summer.

On and on it all went, failure stacked on failure, more despair at every turn of the card. This was mid-August, and as fate would have it, it would all be downhill until December.

What price Russia's sea lane? What price any hope for a defeated Ottoman army? In all of this mess, where does anyone convincingly point a finger? Who knew then? Who knows now? Who will ever know? Dad was there, and he didn't know. Too many secrets. Too little evidence. Too many questions. Too many suspects. Not enough answers. Save your guesses. Gallipoli is the ultimate guessing game. There are too many locked doors. Random stabs at the truth don't count.

AUGUST 17

Another brigade of Tommies landed again last night and have gone up on the left. They must be going to try again. We have had a good day and I know nothing of what happened after 9 o'clock last night till daylight this morning where we stood to.

AUGUST 18

Things were very lively on the left last night, but we were in our dugouts out of the line and don't know what happened. The fire was very heavy during the night but today has been quiet.

AUGUST 19

We relieved the 9th Light Horse Regiment at daylight this morning again at Wilson's Post and things were quiet until 4 o'clock. There was heavy shelling further away on our left.

AUGUST 20

The battle started again on the left last night. The Tommies are at it this time, it has been going all day and the place is on fire. We are not in it this time, just holding our line, and things are fairly quiet around here on our right flank and about time. But we get plenty of shell fire.

The fire Dad mentioned was on Scimitar Hill, a mile or two west of Suvla Bay. It had been started by excessive gun and shell fire that ignited the scrub, and it had been burning for days. The British had managed to take Lala Baba, the hill above the Suvla Bay beach, and from that vantage point, one of the soldiers watched helplessly while the flames of Scimitar Hill spread into rows of wounded men who were forced to crawl, stumble, or roll way from the approaching inferno. Not all of them succeeded. When news of that reached Anzac Cove, it was another head-shaking downer. Would they ever end?

AUGUST 22

The Battle is still very heavy-going on the left and has extended as far as Quinn's Post. They were fighting all night. The scrub on the hills is still on fire and things can be plainly seen for a distance at night. The battleships set more places on fire today. The battle has still been raging all day but has not come any further this way.

AUGUST 22

The Turks opened up a very heavy bombardment on Lone Pine last night and on our trenches. We thought they would get through, but they did not. Our batteries have been shelling them all night and all day today. The battle was raging all night and all day at Quinn's Post and fresh troops have been going up all night.

AUGUST 23

The battle is still going strong at Chocolate Hill but has stopped at Quinn's Post. Things have been fairly quiet there since daylight but the Jackos opened up on us at midnight with heavy fire and we replied with heavy fire back till daylight.

AUGUST 24

The battle has ceased on the left and they did not get what they were after. They lost very heavily after severe fighting. I saw 500 out of one regiment buried in one grave today when we were up with one of our guns, and brought back one of theirs that was out of action. We have to get it fixed. No Australians were in this last battle. The place is a death trap, and some are calling it a slaughter yard.

It's difficult here to understand who "they" are. Assuming my father is referring to the Turks, it must mean they didn't get their way with the "fresh troops." The buried 500 are probably Turkish soldiers, and the gun that was brought back for repairs; "one of theirs" is obviously a Turkish machine gun. Dad says, "*no Australians*" were in the battle, so it must have been fought by the "*fresh troops.*" He's not making things too clear, and his final entries don't say much at all. When Kitty read his diary with him, he admitted that recollections of events in his last entries were hazy; clearer details eluded him; and as he said, he was just too exhausted to think or write anything down.

Draw a blank.

AUGUST 25, 26, 27, 28, 29

Things have been very quiet on both sides since the last battle. Both sides seem to have had enough for a while. We have been in the line all the time, but things have been very quiet, and nothing has occurred to relate.

AUGUST 30 and 31

Still very quiet but things have been lively around Suvla Bay this last two days. Nothing doing at our front: Some of the 2nd has arrived but have not seen them yet.

SEPTEMBER 1

Very heavy shell fire on the left last night and the 2nd Division got the lot of it and lost a lot of men. We had a good deal of shell fire but not much damage.

The relieving 2nd Division arrived from Egypt and walked straight into another firestorm. Dad goes into no detail. He's out of it. The hilly terrain surrounding Anzac Cove is now nothing more than the death trap he referred to in his earlier entry. My father has had enough. He's past caring and past writing. His Gallipoli is past understanding. He can't fathom it anymore. He doesn't want to. He doesn't need to. He's waiting for some kind of end . . .

SEPTEMBER 2, 3, 4, 5, 6, 7, 8, 9

Things have been quiet: Sometimes heavy fire but mostly quiet on all fronts.

THE END OF MY FATHER'S GALLIPOLI

SEPTEMBER 15

I woke up on board the Olympic yesterday and we are on the way to Malta. The last thing I can remember is a sandbag spinning in the air and all I know is that a shell hit the trench just over my head and I know no more. There is not a mark on me, but I have been spitting up blood all day and my head is fit to burst. Since I woke up there are a lot of wounded men on board this ship which is one of the biggest ships afloat.

The end of his days at Anzac Cove had come for Dad. Not the end he expected. Not as soon as expected. Not as bad as it could have been. Against the odds, his luck had held! He didn't know how. He didn't know why. Not then, not ever. It happened. That's all he knew. The *Olympic*; sister ship to the *Titanic*, not as big, was launched two years earlier and was just as luxurious. She had been stripped of her classy appointments and refitted as a hospital transfer ship. Sergeant Charlie Lord was obviously impressed.

SEPTEMBER 25

Have been too sick to write a diary of late but am in Number 1 Australian General Headquarters Cairo and doing well but get awful headaches. I was taken off Gallipoli and did not know my misery came to an end without knowing about it. When I woke up and was lying on a mattress and had pyjamas on, I thought I was dreaming and could not make myself realize I was not. I thought I would wake up in the trenches again. We were well looked after when we came back to hospital. The sisters could not do enough for us.

It was all over: After convalescing for weeks in Egypt, Dad was discharged. He sailed home on one of the troopships. He never saw his Waler again, and didn't connect with Ali. Kitty said she didn't recognise him when he got off the train in Rockhampton.

> "He looked like he'd aged twenty years, and it took him months to return to some kind of normality. He was plagued by nightmares and lack of sleep and there was little I could do to help. It was then I realised that the man who went away had gone forever, and would never come back."

Slowly and surely he began to live again. Rockhampton and Kitty Price did it. But she was right. He was no longer the Charlie Lord who left on the train to fight; the Charlie who rode the ranges, the jackeroo who slept beside his cattle dogs and puffed on roll-your-owns while he told jokes, made up nicknames and laughed because he loved his life, knew who he was, and knew where he belonged.

He never lost love for his country and he never lost sight of his responsibilities. He married Kitty. He adjusted; freely devoting himself to the world he came back to, and to the people who lived in it with him.

But deep inside, Gallipoli never lost its hold. It had taken the young man he'd been and turned him into someone else. I can't say that the *"someone else"* is a lesser man. If anything, I feel he may very well be a wiser man. I didn't know the other one, so I can't say for sure. But I'd take the bet. Kitty realised he'd changed but she was one of the original *for-better-and-for-worse* women of her time. She went on loving Dad no matter which man he was.

In his quieter moments, a strange melancholy took him over and sent sad messages from his eyes. The messages came and went, sadder but softer as his years advanced. Here are the closing words written on the last page of his diary. Most of his final chapter has been said previously in this account, but here's what he wrote.

> *Everything we needed (on Gallipoli) had to be carried up from the beaches to the trenches; about two miles. All this had to be done at night-time, big parties of men had to go down every night and do this work as all our movements*

could be seen from the Turkish positions. Another thing about the Dardanelles was that it did not matter where you were you were always under fire, and it was safer up in the firing line than behind it, as they were always shelling behind the lines. A terrible lot of men were lost that way.

Another great difficulty was shortage of water which had to be brought ashore in barges and carried up at night-time. A lot of times we did not get any, sometimes for eight hours and sometimes longer than that, and all through the very hot months of summer. We got food of a kind, tinned bully beef and hard biscuits, and we got bread once a week, a loaf between four men and fresh meat only once a week. We also got jam and cheese, but the flies were so bad you could not eat any jam if you put it on your biscuit. It would be black with flies before you could get it near your mouth and the cheese was always too strong to eat. We also got an issue of rum twice a week to keep down sickness but there was a lot of it there, and could anyone wonder at it—we often went without washing our faces, and our clothes were walking with lice and we could not get a change or wash them often. There was always an awful stench from the dead that could not be buried. Nobody who was not there could realize what we had to go through. It was worse than words could tell. Everyone looked as if they had been through something terrible. We were dirty and ragged and half-starved. There was always danger.

This has been written by me after Gallipoli was left to the Turks, but my original regiment was landed on May 8, 1915, 650 strong and only 11 men came right through. All the rest were killed, wounded, or left sick, and we had about 600 reinforcements during the time we were there. The new regiment came away only 350 strong (after the 600 reinforcements were added) and all the rest of the battalions were the same. And after all that, it was a failure. I will not say anymore only to thank God I came away safe. I thought it was hopeless many a time as I had so many narrow escapes from death.

GALLIPOLI:
THE LAST GOODBYES

CHARLES BEAN WAS GALLIPOLI'S Ginger Meggs, the do-or-die Aussie war correspondent. He landed at Anzac Cove on April 25, called it home, toughed it out and hung around in his muddy dugout in the cliffs until the long-overdue December retreat. He dug in and saw it all—the battles, the killing, the disappointments, the heartbreak, and the few moments of levity.

He had unyielding respect for the men and the way they endured the unendurable. With a shrug of his skinny frame, he stoutly refused to have a bullet removed from his leg after he'd been shot at Suvla Bay; it would have meant leaving the Peninsula for a few days, so he rested up in his dugout and wore the bullet for the rest of his life. When the long-awaited evacuation of the Peninsula finally began, he made this observation:

> *The uppermost thought in the mind of every man I spoke to, was regret at leaving all the little mountain cemeteries which every valley and hillside contains. For weeks past, at any time of the day, you saw small parties of men carefully lettering the half-obliterated name of some comrade on a rough wooden cross, or carefully raking a mound, and bordering it with fuse caps from fallen shells.*

His words nail the emotions of departing soldiers; final tributes; last goodbyes. With the long prayed-for retreat finally happening in the Gallipoli winter of 1915, men about to be set free from the numbing hell of a war that did nothing for anyone, pause to make neat a last resting place, or to negate the possibility of an unmarked grave.

Corral the thoughts that drove those actions, and clearly identify the heart and soul of the Gallipoli nobody wanted to know, and in some cases, still don't want to know. But despite the new-wave thinking of a newer world, Gallipoli's hold on the emotions of people who can see beyond the darkness of 1915 has grown too strong to be forgotten.

Beneath the crosses that rose in profusion over the hills and valleys of the craggy landscape, there lay the broken bodies of soldiers robbed of their youth; unable to leave anything of themselves but a loving memory behind.

In the early Twentieth Century homes and hearths of Australia and New Zealand, loneliness and sadness smothered the happiness that had once lived there.

The expense of the Dardanelles battles ran deep in terms of hard cash, way deeper in terms of human anguish. It is impossible to believe that the lives of any of the men who paused in pitiful and touching attempts to make a dead comrade seem worthy of a better resting place, could ever be the same.

The wildflowers of Gallipoli that burst into bloom the following spring waved in the wind, adding beauty to the bitter sorrow of lives that ended too soon. The wildflowers of spring still bloom on Gallipoli. Nature has her way of softening things; stirring memories; motivating respect and trapping moments.

The men and women who served on Gallipoli: in the trenches, on the battlefields and in the hospitals, have left something behind, something that goes close to explaining the mysteries of life; the power of love and endurance, and the ultimate emptiness of cynical claims that life is nothing more than it appears to be.

If that's all it is, then why are these lives so valuable, and why are memories of these men and women, and what they did, still so important? Look to Gallipoli for the answer, and witness one of history's ugliest chapters turn into something worth cherishing; and beyond that; something worth acknowledging for the miracle it is.

This is the Gallipoli we celebrate, and for those of us who see it that way, it will always be so honoured— in Great Britain, in the lands of the Empire's Allies, and in the countries of the Southern Cross.

The Gallipoli we know is not about war. It is not about the glorification of war; it's about the glorification of thousands of young men and boys, and of dedicated young women, all of whom gave their dreams and futures to Gallipoli.

They then saw them squandered and lost on the blunders and incompetence of the powerful men pledged to honour them, or thrown away by leaders who were committed to act as guides in their willingness to serve the countries they chose to fight for.

Instead, Gallipoli became the war nobody won, and the passing of decades has not been able to blunt the sharpness of the sword that can never be withdrawn from its bleeding heart.

BOOK TWO

GALLIPOLI: THE AFTERMATH

BY 1919 THE OTTOMAN EMPIRE, seriously weakened by the Dardanelles Campaign, lost control of Constantinople, and it was handed over to the new Turkish Republic. In 1920 Greece went to war with Turkey over ownership of the city and lost the fight. Then, in 1930, the Turkish Republic changed its name to one with a Greek derivation—Istanbul,
Don't try to work that out!
The Russians got into the act by blitzing each other in a Civil War that began in 1917, and ended the Russian Empire in an orgy of persecution and death.

Germany was forced to toe the line for a while after signing the Treaty of Versailles. Great Britain and France finished up with red faces, red bank accounts, and drowning in even redder ink.

David Lloyd George finally copped a barrel of blame for the Gallipoli debacle and was forced to resign four years after the Armistice that was signed on the 11th hour of the 11th day of the 11th month in 1918.

Great Britain and her Allies, including America, were hailed as the winning team of the Dardanelles fiasco. In 1940, by some miracle, or by some inner inferno of determination, Winston Churchill drove himself on to become the godsend of the Second World War; a wordsmith and statesman of wondrous persuasion. He rode the image of a cigar-chomping bulldog who publicly snarled at Adolph Hitler and dared him to set foot on his island home at the risk of courting England's wrath. Although Churchill was demeaned, and still is in some quarters, as a flashy, overstated statesman who conned the world—he constantly rallied war-torn Brits with his famous message of hope; the *"V for Victory"* sign made with the first and middle fingers of his right hand.

Good cheeky stuff!

The man's incredible ballsy performance may have been cynically regarded by his critics, but if he'd been a movie star, Hollywood would have handed him an Oscar. It was eventually handed to film actor Gary Oldman, who portrayed him in *The Darkest Hour* in 2017.

And the winner is . . .

With the Armistice signed, Australia and New Zealand went back to being progressive dominions; its soldiers were honoured as heroes, and Gallipoli took its place in the histories of both countries. America became more American than ever; proudly steeped in the razzle-dazzle of *"Over There,"* the rousing George M Cohan song that had trumpeted the nation's entry into the Great War in 1917.

> *Over there, over there,*
> *Send the word, send the word over there,*
> *That the Yanks are coming, the Yanks are coming,*
> *The drums rum-tumming everywhere.*
> *So prepare, say a prayer,*
> *Send the word, send the word to beware,*
> *We'll be over, we're coming over,*
> *And we won't come back till it's over-over there*

When folks tell you there's no business like showbusiness, this song clearly demonstrates what showbusiness is all about!

A peaceful planet was off to a flying start with the 1920s, thrillingly identified as the most flamboyant decade ever, and appropriately referred to as *"The Roaring Twenties."* The World ran amok. Exuberant times proliferated, and a decade of wild tomorrows rode the rollercoaster. And then, out of the blue, the whole shebang ran off the rails with the shock of October 29, 1929.

Black Tuesday—New York's Wall Street Stock Market crash caught the world in a good-time trap of its own making. High-flying frivolity was killed stone dead, and the door to the gloom of the Great Depression opened—payback time for the hedonistic years of the Roaring Twenties, and beyond bad.

Ruined millionaires dived out of high-rise windows; soup kitchens eclipsed swank restaurants; hobos rode the railroads; families lined up for bread and dripping, and Charlie Chaplin got richer making everyone laugh.

The Twentieth Century turned sour and the world crossed its fingers. 1929 limped into 1930, and the following decade played havoc with everyone as they stumbled around in search of financial stability.

While the world's flummoxed citizens struggled to get back on their feet, few failed to notice the dark shadows rising over

Germany, a proud country still smouldering over defeat in the Great War, and whose industrial future was wiped out by the Great Depression.

Adolf Hitler rose to power in the thirties and the hopes of the German people rose with him. By the end of the decade, Hitler held Europe in his grip, but Europe was not enough. He wanted Great Britain and its Empire, and just like his buddies in the first Great War, he wanted the world; all if it.

His timing was perfect. While the entire planet was recovering from its money problems, Germany had become a hungry monster driven by the will of the ultimate egomaniac. *Another mortal storm was shaping up.*

Deaf ears had ignored the warnings of the prophets who had identified Hitler as dangerous as far back as 1932. When the war finally came, as the prophets said it would, it hit with a sickening thud on Friday the 1st of September 1939. Great Britain and France, the military twins of the First Great War, shirt-fronted Hitler after he barged into Poland, and dared him to back off.

He didn't, and the shackles went up on both sides.

Once again America stood still, but the British Dominions were stirred into the pot and they rallied. The populations of Australia and New Zealand prepared for what they knew was coming. In all of this, the ghosts of Gallipoli lingered in Australia and New Zealand, and inspired young men to do what their fathers and grandfathers had done in 1915.

"It's on again, fellas; up and at 'em!"

DAD'S LAST POST

My father was in no physical condition for another Gallipoli.

He'd been following the news on the wireless and he didn't like it at all. The 1930s had not been good to him. He married Kitty after he came home from Gallipoli, and they invested in a timber mill in a small town south of Rockhampton. The building industry had taken off and Queensland was on the move.

Two of Dad's brothers were in the business with him and they gave it heaps of muscle and sweat as the twenties rolled away.

Then the Depression clobbered Australia. The building industry collapsed, and the timber mill went broke. Dad said, *"Well, we didn't win that one,"* and moved us to Bundaberg—Kitty, me and my older sisters, Dorothy, and Lexie—*Team Charlie*.

Bundaberg spelled sugar. Big time sugar! Dad scored a gig in the cane fields; hard work for a Gallipoli veteran, but we had to eat. Then he got a break.

A turn as an overseer in the engine room of the massive Bundaberg Sugar Refinery landed in his lap. Better job, more money.

Kitty could make apple pies and custard again.

Then one stormy afternoon in 1937, the Refinery's big brick chimney took a hit from a lightning bolt and caught fire. Exploding barrels of rum turned the fire into an inferno. Rum gushed into the Burnett River, the fumes from the fire turned the moon blue, and all the fish got drunk. Dad was out of work until everything could all be rebuilt.

The cane fields weren't an option, but his experience with machinery set him up for a position in the brand new Butter Factory in Biloela.

Team Charlie had never heard of Biloela, but Dad found it somewhere south-west of Gladstone, with unsealed roads, a train station, one main street, kerosene lamps, a telephone exchange, and an open-air picture theatre. I watched *Snow White and the Seven Dwarfs* in the rain—twice.

Two years later, Dad scored a better gig in charge of the Powerhouse at Monto, a crackerjack agricultural town some miles south of Biloela.

Monto had sealed streets, a bigger train station, electric lights, two pubs, two cafes, malted milks, and an indoor picture theatre with canvas seats. Dad took me to see *Rose Marie* to hear Jeanette MacDonald and Nelson Eddy sing "*The Indian Love Call.*" I told him I liked it. Yeah, but I liked *The Northwest Mounted Police* better. Gary Cooper was in that—*in Technicolor*

Right about now, the war in Europe was getting nasty and Dad was getting edgy. Hitler was on the move. His troops were running wild in North Africa, The Battle for Britain was on, and German bombs rained on London every night.

At home, the young lads of Monto were enlisting to fight with the famous *Rats of Tobruk* and in the Royal Australian Air Force. Australia revved up:

The enlisting boys left with the blessings of the town with a watch and a wallet. The farewell speeches were keyed by the Maori Farewell; *Now is the hour when we must say goodbye.* Monto's mothers wept.

That kind of stuff got to Dad, especially when he shook the hands of the enlisting boys. Fateful telegrams arrived much faster in Monto than they had during the Gallipoli war—scores of Monto's young men would not be coming home.

Mum and Dad were coping with tragic news of their own. My elder sister Lexie had been fatally injured in a car crash on the range between Biloela and Monto on Saturday, November 25, 1939.

Charlie and Kitty moved on, but the sadness lingered; touchingly at times; long moments of silence and restless nights, easy to see that something wonderful had gone from our lives.

The war news kept coming: Spitfires over London ripping into the Luftwaffe, the small-boats rescue of British troops trapped on the beaches of Dunkirk, the RAF's thousand-bomber raid on Cologne, the mysterious disappearance of HMAS Sydney, and the stalking and sinking of the German battleship, *Bismark*; big news that interrupted the screening of the motion picture, *Ships with Wings*' at the Monto picture theatre. Cheers when the news was flashed on the screen. *I was there with Dad.*

For as long as the war was contained in the northern hemisphere, he was calm. Mum joined local women in a rightly-named "Comfort Club," long hours knitting scarves, socks, and sweaters to be forwarded to Brisbane, then to the battle zones of Europe and Africa. My father's droning engines at the Powerhouse were keeping Monto supplied with electric lights. His two assistants had enlisted, and he was a one-man band. His hours were long, but his ear was never far away from the nightly bulletins on the wireless.

Things unexpectedly got worse.

While Monto's business people were attaching decorated gum tree branches to awnings in the main street for the war's third Christmas, news of the Japanese attack on the American Fleet in Pearl Harbor on December 7, 1941, scrambled the town.

A trembling Australia held its breath. Dad didn't sleep.

America declared war on Japan.

In February 1942 more Japanese bombs fell on Darwin than on Pearl Harbor. Two hundred people died. Three months later the Battle of the Coral Sea brought the war to Queensland. The ladies in Mum's Comfort Club took to weaving heavy balls of twine into camouflage nets for the town's buildings.

A team of soldiers dug zig-zag trenches in the grounds of the Monto State School where us kids were drilled in the fastest way to get into them and how to stay out of the way of bullets from enemy planes.

We thought it was fun.

The windows of Monto's houses were criss-crossed with adhesive brown paper to prevent injury from flying glass in case of air raids; heavy curtains hung over windows to cut the glow of after-dark lights visible from the sky. At dusk every day, Dad dimmed the power to the town's street lights, and stood by to turn them off if we were raided.

In the South Pacific, Japanese armies were on the move. Hong Kong fell. Singapore fell. The Philippines fell. The Japanese moved on the Solomon Islands and New Guinea. Charlie was sleepless.

The government began a steady evacuation of women and children from the Queensland seaboard to smaller, safer towns in the country. Monto took its share. My father's worry peaked when he was told by Police Sergeant Seth Caton (actor Michael Caton's father) that signs on the town's businesses, railway station, hotels and banks were to be painted over to remove the word "Monto" in a bid to prevent an invading enemy from knowing exactly where they were.

Seth punched the point home: "We're on notice, Charlie, and we've got to start painting right away."

That did it. Dad hit the panic button. The old warhorse, at fifty-three, made his move. He had discovered that the Powerhouse on the Brisbane River at Doboy, a plant that serviced half the city, had a labour crisis caused by the departure of enlisting men. He took the train to Brisbane, got a grateful response from the Doboy management, landed a job as an engine supervisor, and found a place for us to live in the bayside suburb of Wynnum North, ten minutes away from Doboy in the train.

Dad came home to Monto and said, "If the enemy comes, they'll need towns like this to feed them, and we'll be done for. Pack what we can take, leave what we can't. We're heading off tomorrow on the Rail Motor."

We spent Christmas by the sea in Wynnum North and Dad took over the Doboy Powerhouse.

Brisbane resembled the train crash in the *Greatest Show on Earth*.

The American Fleet had sailed in from The Coral Sea and it was "Hello Sailor." The American Air Force had taken over Doomben Racecourse to build a major airport. GI camps had mushroomed all over the outer suburbs.

Cloudland Ballroom was an American Army administration Centre, and several upmarket residences close to the airport billeted military heavies and functioned as executive offices. Aussie soldiers roamed the streets with tens of thousands of free-spending Yanks. The CBD was non-stop rock and roll.

Movies played to packed houses. *Casablanca* ran for over a year. Pop Bands went decibel crazy with the sounds of Tommy Dorser and Glenn Miller in the dance halls. Massive Cement air raid shelters went up on city streets, Douglas Macarthur, the "*I Shall Return*" General set up his executive centre in an eight-story city building, and slept with his wife and son in Lennons Hotel.

The pubs were limited to short two-hourly sessions every day, black-market booze made hucksters rich, and the madams of the pleasure pits made enough cash to live like royalty after the war.

An incredible brittle glamour pervaded the town. The threat of an enemy invasion caused the outbreak of a *what-if-tomorrow-never-comes fever*.

It's now or never was the name of the game.

It accelerated with the sinking off Moreton Island of the *Centaur*, a hospital ship headed for Brisbane. A well-aimed torpedo hit the target. Over two hundred wounded soldiers, medical staff, nurses, and offices went down in flames. The city reeled in shock. If one enemy submarine was out there, how many more could there be?

At Doboy, Charlie was on blackout standby every night. At the lookouts the American Army Airport swept the skies for low-flying bombers.

Brisbane became the city that never sleeps.

Charlie was locked in his post. If he left, who'd replace him? He made plans to move us into the basement boiler rooms of the Powerhouse if the bombing started.

> *"Let's get ready with plenty of stuff to eat and drink. This is going to get nasty. I can smell it coming."*

Then out of nowhere, the shock of the atomic bomb wipe-out of Hiroshima in 1945 ricocheted around the world and bounced into Brisbane.

Suddenly, everything changed.

As everyone guessed, the dropping of the second atom bomb on Nagasaki sealed Japan's doom. The end was on its way.

"Peace!" screamed the Brisbane *Telegraph* headline on Wednesday, August 15, 1945. Brisbane's inner city erupted in showers of shredded paper, fluttering confetti, and streamers. We were dismissed from school to spend the day yelling and skylarking until midnight in Queen Street like everyone else.

Came the dawn of Thursday, August 16, and it was all over.

In the flick of the eye, Brisbane's brittle glitter evaporated; it just went away. An eerie emptiness took its place and hung in the air for months. The lights and neon signs came back, but the buzz had gone. Not for Charlie. At the age of 56, he settled back into his life after having lived through two of the greatest conflicts in the history of the planet.

He hated being idle and never stopped working: When he was 75, he took on the supervision of an air-conditioning plant in a corporate building at Brisbane's North Quay, his last job. After filling in reams of official forms, he was denied a wounded veterans pension, and took it philosophically.

> *"It would have been nice, but I never did it for the money."*

I knew my father for the kind of man he was, just an ordinary bloke who took life on when the going got tough. I remember him well. I will never forget him. He lived with me every day of my life—he still does.

Wartime Brisbane looms like a mirage in my mind, a blurred picture of high excitement; days and nights of hedonistic nervous energy. I was a just a curious impressionable kid from the sticks living in a kind of reckless grown-up world; a magic world I had never seen before and will never see again.

GALLIPOLI 2015
THE ANZAC HUNDRED YEAR COMMEMORATIVE

I WASN'T SURE I WAS ready for this adventure, but when I thought more about it, it seemed like a good idea that my son, Kelly Lord urged me to consider. So I did. The Hundred Year Commemorative at Anzac Cove was promoted in Canberra as Gallipoli 2015; a gesture of respect welcomed across the nation.

On-site space for the Dawn Service was limited, so it was expected that close relatives of the original Anzacs were to be given preference: As a first-generation descendant of a Gallipoli veteran, I applied for a ballot, copped a nod, and my son Kelly came with me to make sure I didn't fall out of the stand.

The facts were clear: Anzac Cove is a Turkish National Park, kept and maintained in its natural state. No running water. No shelter from the elements. No permanent food outlets. Possible below-zero temperatures. Dress for the cold. Prepare for rain. Ponchos only. No umbrellas. No alcohol. No drunks. Take everything you need including water. Expect to walk long distances. Prepare for hours in queues to enter the site and long over-night hours waiting for the Dawn Service. Add another eight hours for the Lone Pine Ceremony the day after Anzac Day, and another six hours for the trip back to Istanbul: Total: 36 hours with not much sleep; if any.

The promises: Turkish Food Booths with coffee and tea: Avenues of Portable Toilets. First Aid and Medical Assistance. Abundant on-site supervision:

> *A Once in a Lifetime Experience: A Night to Remember!*

The rules: Take your chances, accept the conditions, and clam up. That's it!

It's no secret that Gallipoli generates permanent income for the Turkish government, which is why truckloads have been spent to preserve its graves, foster its legends, prohibit any commercial development, and enhance it just enough to polish any rough edges. Gallipoli is Turkey's most profitable Theme Park.

It's not referred to as one but that's what it is.

Like the Dardanelles Campaign, Gallipoli 2015 could never happen again.

In Australia, anticipation rode in with the New Year, and rose to a peak in early April: Television, movies, the print media, the Internet, and Anzac hype kept the excitement happening. It was everywhere.

Persistent critics bleated the same three wise words: *"Gallipoli Glorifies War."*

They sounded profound—widely quoted in smart circles where the Hundredth Commemorative was talked down as a sentimental festival for the gullible.

But out there in the streets, in schools, in churches, in towns, in pubs and in people's hearts, the ANZAC spirit prevailed and Gallipoli 2015 took off as the event of the year.

Air travel to Turkey from all over the world ramped up in the week of April 21. Flights from Australia and New Zealand were booked solid, and extra flights were scheduled. Gallipoli 2015 was living up to its promise.

THE MAGIC OF ISTANBUL

THE GREAT CITY, STEEPED IN history, is the stepping stone to the Gallipoli Peninsula. There was a problem in April 2015. Ataturk, Istanbul's International Airport, was in the throes of a major reinvention to increase its size, and was hardly welcoming. Passenger fingers from aircraft to terminal were down, and its other services were below par. My son, who flew in from Paris, arrived before me on April 20. I flew in from Singapore the day after, landed in heavy rain, clattered down the mobile stairs to the tarmac and sprinted to a shuttle bus for a rocky ten-minute ride to the terminal. Waiting time in passport queues was sixty minutes. But this was Gallipoli 2015: Moaning and whingeing weren't on.

By the time we'd cleared airport protocol, the rain had stopped, and the first wow factor of the pilgrimage burst open like a Christmas cracker:

Istanbul was a visual sensation.

The fifty-minute ride from Ataturk International Airport to the city was a gobsmack. Millions of poppies, planted to bloom in April 2015 were living palettes of colour in roadside gardens, in parks, in windows boxes, and in planters on pavements. Living floral murals decorated scores of hoardings.

Beyond lay the sweeping waterway of the Harbour of the Golden Horn, thick with boats and swirling with sea traffic.

Everything was messy, cluttered, intriguing, dazzling, and fascinating, split down the middle by the natural canal of the Bosphorus: Asia on one side, Europe on the other, each side marked by relative architecture. Mosques littered the cityscape. Slender towers with pointed turrets stabbed the sky. Ancient buildings revealed echoes of Constantinople as it was when Winston Churchill wanted to steal it and give it to Russia.

Istanbul's central heart is Taksim on the European side, a long wide plaza that never sleeps; a feverish concourse that shares trams, cars, scooters and vans with people: alluring young women in sweaters, coats, scarves and knee boots; young men with dark wavy hair in leather boots and slim jeans; sleek older men of the word in leather jackets; glamorous older women with knowing eyes in faux fur coats and hats; an ever-moving picture of flesh and fantasy. Where they're going nobody knows, nobody tells, and nobody cares.

Taksim's energy; contagious: Fashion boutiques, furniture stores, restaurants, specialty food stores and eye-catching shops with display windows filled with platters of exotic sweets and lip-smacking Turkish Delight—*the real thing!*

Gallipoli 2015 posters and Turkish flags were everywhere.

Messy tiny streets and lanes are Taksim's concourse tributaries; lined with secret cafes, striped awnings, pavement chairs, tiny tables, and Turkish ice cream shops. Kebab hucksters shout for attention with revolving barrels of roasting chicken, lamb, beef, and boxes of fresh pomegranates cut and squeezed to order: a movie waiting to be filmed.

At night Taksim surrenders to joyful visual orgies of glittering fairy lights. Its heartbeat dims but never dies.

Life is endless: In Taksim, tomorrow never comes.

High on the European shores of the Bosphorus are the mansions of the rich. Manhattan-like towers of modern hotels share space with decorative vintage apartment buildings; ornate and proud; well-preserved messages from the past. Balconies, terraces, windows, and glassy penthouse sky-decks look down on the sparkling water of the Bosphorus where the water is always blue: Above it, white seabirds float around against the blaze of a pollution-free sky.

The hotel where my son and I stayed was in narrow side street with equally narrow sidewalks on either side; food and novelty shops, small restaurants and convenience stores that sell everything for the right price.

We settled in as part of the tour-bus team of twenty-five - Aussies and Kiwis up and down the age scale from various walks of life; light-hearted, and Anzac-eager with a sense of humour. Our tour guide was a well-informed answer machine who knew what the questions would be.

Istanbul's must-sees are the Blue Mosque, the Topkapi Palace, Hagia Sophia, the Spice Markets and a cruise on the Bosphorus. We took a one-day look.

When we arrived at the Mosque with other busloads, it wasn't raining but the sky was heavy. Street-smart hustlers chanting "Aussie-Aussie" were selling see-through plastic umbrellas for 10 lire (about $5). Ten minutes later when the rains came, the price went up to 25 lire (about $12). *Good business!*

The Blue Mosque walk-through has rules: No shoes; no caps or hats for blokes, covered heads for women; scarves supplied if necessary: Line up; gawk and gasp in wet socks at the intoxicatingly intricate blue tiles. Put your shoes back on standing up in a chattering mob of 500, then squelch around the Palace gardens in a sea of umbrellas. Even in the rain, Topkapi was a crowd grabber, simply because no one living today can understand how it ever existed and functioned.

The Spice Markets: a sprawling network of crammed walkways undercover and overwhelming. Think of something you don't need but can't help buying—it's there: Food, fashion, trinkets, pistachio nuts, stuff you've never seen before, and baubles, bangles, and beads; *Irresistible.*

On the outdoor stairways of The Spice Markets are the beggars. Mothers and dirty children with sad eyes and hungry faces: Nobody looks. If so, you're gone. What can anyone do?

Istanbul's world-famous fish sandwiches are thrown together on fishing boats moored on the nearby shores of the harbour. Chunks of unbuttered bread casually wrapped around slabs of boiled fish. Yeah, well; *just like in 007 movies!*

Our knockout cruise up and down the Bosphorus was like sailing through the pages of history and trying not to blink. Two hours of conflicting architecture Asia on one side, vintage decorative Turkey on the other.

Head-turning, literally; even more delicious if you're fanging out on proper Turkish Delight! Istanbul was irresistible foreplay.

THE REAL REASON FOR THE TRIP

THE TOUR BUS JOURNEY FROM Istanbul to the Gallipoli Peninsula revved off at 7 a.m. on April 23 for five-and-a-half hours on the road. Turkish tour buses are flash, smooth, and comfortable with heaps of space, legroom and wide-wide windows. As the outer suburbs of Istanbul slipped away, the astonishing beauty of the countryside took over. The highway hugs the sparsely populated shores of the beautiful Sea of Marmara for three hours: *Time flies.*

There are no toilets on Turkish buses. Fifteen-minute comfort stops were the order of the journey—*take the break or bust*! By arrangements with the tour companies, the comfort stops occur at scheduled places, all catering to several buses at a time. The rush for the loos is Speedy Gonzales.

A special fee of two lire (seventy-five Oz cents) gets you in the line-up. Pay up or don't pee. The attendants don't have change. They're all fans of *Goldfinger* and there's no money-back guarantee.

At the very top of the Dardanelles, our bus entered the Gallipoli Peninsula and scooted past heaps of little villages and farms to reach the captivating little town of Eceabat, located on the dazzling middle eastern seaboard of the Dardanelles Narrows—*you're allowed to gasp.*

Eceabat is the front door to Anzac Cove, a few miles to the east via a narrow road that meanders and bumps over tricky terrain to its famous destination. To ease the stress of heavy traffic on the narrow road, the Turks promised to dig two underground tunnels from Eceabat to Anzac Cove but ran out of time—or something.

The tunnels didn't happen. We didn't care.

Eceabat looks directly across the Dardanelles Narrows to the exotic city of Çanakkale in Asian Turkey. Massive ferry boats that can take up to twenty buses cruse the Narrows to Çanakkale in thirty minutes. If you.re feeling thirsty, you can chill out in the bar.

We bussed into at Eceabat from Istanbul at 1:20 p.m., in time for a sunny Turkish barbecue on a huge wide terrace beside the Dardanelles. There was a surprise: *The loos were free:* Everybody went, and saved money.

The day was bright, sunny; and pleasantly chilly; not cold, with crystal clear views up and down the rippling blue water. Happy locals and their kids were on the ball selling souvenirs, trinkets, flags, fake medals, caps, and sashes.

Saying no was hardly an option.

Aussie TV reporters asked predictable questions and copped predictable answers: Everything was: *"marvellous, exciting, incredible, awesome, mind-blowing and unforgettable." As a matter of fact, everything was.*

After lunch, we hit the road for our first look at what everyone had come to see.

Expectation made the trip too long.

At the end of the ride, the bus stopped on a narrow winding sealed road on the eastern shore of Gallipoli Peninsula—*And there it was:*

Anzac Cove sat in the afternoon sun looking like a sports stadium on the eve of a big match. Rising above the familiar curve of the pebble beach were the famed cliffs of the Cove dominated by the huge rocky outcrop of the Sphinx, every bit as high and mighty as it had been a hundred years ago when my father had been there.

It took a few moments to fit the bright eye candy into the dark mind images if what had happened there so long ago. It's like Nature had waved a wand to make the horrors disappear. They didn't; not quite; not for me.

Gallipoli's glory is elevated by its physical beauty and its power to touch the untouchable. The cemeteries, close by, are well cared for, names clearly visible on polished headstones

The site layout for the Dawn Service was basic: High tiers of orange seats sitting side-on to the Aegean Sea—overlooking a central grassy court backed by more stands set against the towering cliffs, and facing the sea. Closer to the beach were two more stands for VIPs, a smaller grassy court, the presentation stage; lighting and audio towers, plus three enormous audio-visual screens. Several long rows of portaloos completed the set-up.

There were entrances and exits to narrow sealed bitumen roads on either side of the Cove. Beside the main entrance were check-in marquees. Curious minds wondered why the stands couldn't have a protective covering.

The answer is that any kind of covering could inhibit the Cove's arresting physical presence and mask the light of dawn rising over the Aegean Sea.

After the Cove site inspection, we bussed up to Lone Pine, then on to the high ground of Chunuk Bair, which overlooks the shoreline panorama of Anzac Cove, Lone Pine, the infamous Suvla Bay, and the surrounding sweep of the Aegean Sea.

A living page in a spellbinding history book

Lone Pine's one tree; not the original, stands as a monument to one of Gallipoli's most infamous battles. Nobody spoke too much. The sounds of silence said it all.

Thoroughly appropriate.

We returned to Eceabat for a twilight barbecue then took the ferry to the Çanakkale. There, our overnight accommodation at a comfortable hotel had been surrendered to a last-minute team of VIPs. The alternative was two hours away at a run-down seaside resort. *Bit of a downer. We managed.*

At 7:30 a.m. next morning we headed off to eyeball Troy, an hour away. The ancient city is a massive pile of rocks; rocky steps up, rocky steps down to rocky paths; heaps of maps and informative reads, and a fake Trojan horse:

Real-life rock and roll—people everywhere.

Brad Pitt wasn't there. Half the world was.

We were on the wrong side of the Dardanelles. It was way past eleven o'clock on the eve of Anzac Day; *the eve of D-Day!* Spiffy luxury cruise ships were anchored off shore, but there were long bus queues at all the ferry crossings. The question: how do we make it to the right side of the Dardanelles in time for the big night? *No worries.*

Our bus driver was Knightrider. He roared all the way up the thirty-mile Asian side of the waterway to an accommodating northern ferry service that sported a short bus queue. We crossed over, then roared down the Turkish side of the waterway and swept into Eceabat at dusk.

Loud applause and verbal bouquets for the Knightrider.

After one more Eceabat barbecue, we were off!

THE ICEMAN COMETH

WE STOKED UP ON PACKETS of chips, nuts, and bottled water, boarded the bus and headed for the narrow winding road to Anzac Cove:

Thrills ran up and down the bus. Honestly. It was not fake fascination!

We arrived at woody Mimoza Park in the southern surrounds of Anzac Cove and copped the tour guide's brief: We would not see the bus again until the end of the Lone Pine Service which was programmed to finish about 2 p.m. on April 25, at least twenty hours later. We were given the listed number of our bus (eighty-five) and told where to wait after the Lone Pine Ceremony.

Our guide wished us luck and said goodbye.

No bus. No guide. No team. Just us and thousands of Anzac groupies.

At 6:30 p.m. April 24, woody Mimoza Park buzzed like shopping centre on Christmas eve. Guides and attendants, mostly young Aussies, Kiwis and Brits in their twenties, were excited, prepared, all-knowing and helpful. My son and I were among the first to enter the Anzac Cove enclosure. We claimed two seats on the edge of the fourth top row of the stand with a dress circle view of the Cove and the main grass enclosure. To our right was the presentation stage. A giant audio-visual screen erected above the opposite stand was staring right at us. *Perfect!*

The bucket seats were bucket seats. Legroom minimal. We were dressed in layers of warm clothes, beanies, scarves, and gloves. Our bags held bottles of water, rugs and all the necessary stuff. Kits handed out at the entrance included ponchos, beanies, and an information booklet.

There we were set to sit until 7 a.m. on Anzac Day—*daunting? A bit.*

The atmosphere in our stand was *all good, mate.* People of all ages we didn't know and will probably never see again, were our new best friends and neighbours—mostly Aussies and Kiwis; all keyed-it, all chirpy, all rugged up, stuff all over the narrow aisles and more stuff shoved under seats—ultimate togetherness. Being there was worth all the trouble it had taken to get there.

As twilight fell, the sun disappeared over the crags and valleys behind us, and Anzac Cove lit up. Gold spotlights hit the Sphinx high above us. More spotlights were trained on the high hill where Dad's trench had been.

I could see it clearly; hard to look away.

The long night hit the "go" button.

The event's compere was a young bloke who was determined to get it right. He opened with the old *"make-em-happy routine"* Ask the audience the cliché question. *"Are we all happy?"* The answer is never loud enough, so the question is repeated until the answer is a roar. The flavour of the event was thus pigeon-holed as rowdy Music Hall. Corny and clumsy but nobody seemed to mind. *There were no chook raffles.*

Included in the night-long program were the following:

A medley of World War 1 songs by the Australian New Zealand Military Band, a presentation by the Maori Cultural Group, a welter of pre-recorded documentaries about regiments and men who fought at the Cove, Lone Pine and Chunuk Bair; stories about the nurses on the hospital ships, performances by the Gregory Terrace-All Hallows' Gallipoli Choir from Brisbane, Live readings of Gallipoli Tributes by three prize-winning Australian students, a student reading to honour the bearer of New Zealand's VC award, recorded interviews with living descendants, and Jack Thompson's entire nine-part documentary series: *Gallipoli: The Untold Stories* recorded in 2005, and repeatedly played on Australian television every April since.

Familiar but fitting

Shortly after midnight, our compere announced that 2,500 extra people were being admitted to the site, and that they were to be accommodated on the grassy courts, which were already filled. To cope with the crush, he made it clear that people occupying grass space could no longer be seated or stretched out in sleeping bags. Our view of the escalating crush from our dress circle seats was not a good look. The Kiwi behind me said, *"Real-life sardines."* New people kept pouring in until they were standing shoulder to shoulder on the grass.

The promised Turkish Food Vendors slated to be operating until 3 a.m., ran out of food, coffee, and tea by 11 p.m. *There were no riots.* The infamous portaloos closest to our stand lost both their interior and exterior lighting around midnight when traffic was heavy. Mob rule prevailed.

The sweet little lady in front of me in the next row said:

"It took me ten minutes to get out of all this warm clobber and when I did, I couldn't see the seat." The whole row cracked up!

The hours rolled on. Around 3:30 a.m. an icy chill stole over Anzac Cove and crept into the very bones of the heavily rugged thousands in the public stands, and those standing shoulder to shoulder on the grassy courts. Everyone had been warned about the extreme weather and here it was, biting us. We took it on the chin and shivered. No moans. No complaints. No regrets. A few comments:

"Jeez, they were right about the weather, cobber. It's sure is bloody cold."

As the dim glow of the approaching dawn fell over the waters of the Aegean Sea, the patrolling battleships came into view in the middle distance, and the clear water of the Anzac Cove beach was illuminated in the glow of strategically placed blue lights.

Above the beach, the softly lit folds of the rugged hills and rocky towers heralded the imagined arrival of the ghosts of the 11th Anzac Battalion; as fresh and young as they'd been on that morning that had dawned, so icy and still, exactly one hundred years before. If moments can be magic, those moments were. Not a sound anywhere.

The beach was the same, the rocky cliffs were the same, the Aegean Sea was the same. The bullets and blood, banished by the soul power of the silent crowd, weren't there. Anzac Cove had no place for them that morning.

Every face in the crowd was turned toward the beach, and the weather suddenly didn't seem cold anymore. It didn't matter that the food stalls and loos broke down, that the Music Hall host was way off-key or that the crush of people on the grassy court was a pain in the butt. This was no place to be pinging off at the Anzac Legend. You'd have had a better chance of howling down the Indians at Custer's Last Stand.

Dad didn't land on April 25 in 1915, his arrival was two weeks later when the rot had set in, but he sure was in the stand with me in 2015; so were the men and boys who fought with him. If you didn't believe in miracles, you were on the wrong bus.

At home in the autumn warmth of Oz, it was thirty minutes past midnight, two hours earlier in NZ. What was happening for real on the Gallipoli Peninsula was beamed into hundreds of thousands of television sets at home.

Dawn Services played early that year. If you're an ANZAC groupie in Oz and NZ you're on the right brick road.

The Cove's Live Dawn Service began on the dot of 5:30 a.m. and the crowd yawned, stretched, and woke up. The highlights:

Brit Royals airlifted from Çanakkale by helicopter to Eceabat then limo-driven to the Cove turned up; Prince Charles, as imperious as ever, wrapped his fruity plum-ripened vowels around well-written sentences like he always does—*a royal performance, beautifully intoned*

Prince Harry, fresh, young, and joyfully preppy, looking and sounding nothing like the pontificating vigilante he's turned into, invested his words with the thoughtful awe of youth, and the punters loved him.

The familiar tone of the event was enlivened by the speech delivered by the then New Zealand Prime Minister Jon Key, all fire and verbal precision, every word and sentence perfectly framed, every emotion forcefully projected.

Wonderful!

Stepping up to the stand in his wake—Australia's then Prime Minister Tony Abbott. A murmur of concern rippled through the nearby Australians in our stand. We knew Tony was no orator. A tentative silence hung over the site. The cameras caught him in close-up, and he launched into his address.

No pauses; no stuttering; steady eyes; none of the usual self-conscious pauses. He was looking good and sounding even better, but the best was yet to come: It wasn't a long speech, but it ended with a touching passage about how the selflessness and moral courage of men and women in all wars are held forever in our thoughts and hearts. It ended with this:

"They did their duty; now let us do ours."

Prime Minister Abbott had surely been tutored and coached by someone who knew how it was done, but give him his due: it was his speech, and it rang bells.

A rousing response from the crowd!

The rest of the show was painless, held together with care and proper respect for the cause - choirs, songs, prayers, and the glorious notes of the trumpeted *Last Post* soaring out over Anzac Cove in goose-pimpling echoes of remembrance. A once in a lifetime happening had come to an end.

THE EXIT FROM THE SITE was masterfully organised. Section by section was vacated in sequence: Standing crowds on the grass were followed by the people in the stands moving row by row.

Nobody broke the flow. Elated Gallipoli groupies, lugging bags and other clutter, played the rules. The site cleared in thirty minutes.

Coming up in four hours: Lone Pine.

No sleep. No breakfast. No coffee. No Banana Smoothies. No Corn Flakes. Nobody looked tired. No kidding, no one –*Pack up your troubles in your old kit bag and smile, smile, smile.*

It's hard to believe that only five short years later, that the twentieth decade of Planet Earth's Twenty-First Century is being attacked by angry social threats to tear down the established worlds of the past. Aggravation, brittle thinking, hard-edged words, and feverish hollering have taken to the streets, and desperate people morph into snarling bullies to grab for what they think they want, and what they say we should have.

None of that showed its ugly face at the Anzac Commemorative or on in the Down Under ANZAC lands of Australia and New Zealand when flickering candles in the driveways of home held any new wave anger at bay but the future is still in the winds of tomorrow.

Twelve thousand pilgrims and a hundred thousand reasons to remember every moment.
Anzac turns 100

Audio-Visual Screen

Blue water on the beach

LONE PINE IN THE SUN

As the crow flies, Lone Pine is close south-west of Anzac Cove over steep hills and craggy valleys. Easiest access: Walk half a mile south on the road that hugs the shore, then head west along a continually steep track that winds west for another mile to the Lone Pine Memorial.

Alerted that the ragged track was a challenging trek, even for daredevils, several took it on with dire results and had to be treated by the First Aid crew. Smarter hikers chose to amble south along the beach road, skirt the low hills and valleys then double back and head north to Lone Pine; a longer hike that took over an hour; a long pull after a hard night. My son Kelly conquered the daredevil track. I scored a seat in one of the special shuttle buses on the beach road for the ten-minute drive to Lone Pine. *Limmo service.*

By 9:30 a.m. most of the Australian contingent had arrived at the site for the 11 a.m. service. New Zealanders had to walk for a further hour north for the early afternoon service at Chunuk Bair.

After a cramped and sleepless night, it was a relief to be able to move and walk. Morning hikes, even short ones to the shuttle buses, were pleasant.

Not so pleasant: *hunger had set in.*

Lone Pine was no catered picnic. No more than 10 stalls sold lazy food: biscuits, chocolate bars, mints, and the ubiquitous packets of chips. Coffee if you were lucky. Officials handed out free bottles of water; unconsciously triggering trips to the Lone Pine portaloos, which were even more frightening in daylight than the night-time models at the Cove, but the predicted rain didn't fall.

The stands were comfortable and pleasant in the chilly morning sun. To make sure we were happy, our Music Hall compere from the night before kept us on our toes by being a Music Hall compere.

The Buckingham Palace Princes, Charles and Harry, arrived with the other officials, then performed a meet-and-greet with the hordes in the stands. Harry was mobbed. Charles wasn't, but he automatically nodded and grinned like he always does.

The hour-long service was a repeat of the Dawn Service with places, names and events changed. Tony Abbott gave out again. Mrs Abbott, sleek and fashionable in black, laid a wreath on the monument. The leader of the opposition, Bill Shorten, read passages from the Bible, and told us we should always forgive our trespassers and turn the other cheek. *Yes, well...*

He laid a wreath on the monument, and the service ended.

High Noon on Anzac Day 2015.

The official program made it clear that we'd have to wait until the conclusion of the New Zealand Service at Chunuk Bair—just up the road—before the buses from Eceabat could begin to creep up the narrow road up to Lone Pine.

No food. No snacks. No chips. No biscuits. Plenty of water: Lots of trips to the portaloos: *The Marx Brothers at the Circus.*

Spent pilgrims spread out on the grass and got into trouble for stepping over headstones on the graves. 4 p.m. came and went. No buses.

4:40 p.m. Buses were on the way; *cheers*! As they reached Lone Pine, their numbers flashed up on audio-visual screens. Passenger pick-ups at Lone Pine and Chunuk Bair went ahead. Next stop: Istanbul.

Hundreds of buses moved at a snail's pace up the narrow road from Eceabat. Time crawled. There were no tantrums. *She's apples, mate. It's Anzac.*

6:45 p.m.: Our bus arrived. We'd been at Lone Pine for ten hours. By the time we'd picked up our New Zealanders at Chunuk Bair, it was 7:15 p.m. We hit the road to Istanbul in comfortable seats in a big warm bus. *Heaven.*

Arrival time in Istanbul was 1:20 a.m. on April 26. We and had to be packed and ready to leave for the Ataturk Airport by 9 a.m. the next day for a flight to Singapore at 11 a.m. We made it; with six boxes of proper Turkish Delight to spare.

Our Gallipoli 2015 was history.

LOOKING BACK

COMMEMORATIVE VISITORS TO GALLIPOLI WERE well-informed about the risks of attendance. Canberra could smell trouble coming from a mile away, so all bases were covered by frequent reminders about conditions at Anzac Cove. Canberra had no control over the Turkish Food Vendors who under-performed, the Turkish loos that under-functioned, or the decision to admit thousands of late-comers to the site.

Canberra did have control over the night's "nostalgic and reflective" program and they messed up with the Music Hall fluff and the night's lack of "wow factors." But the event spoke for itself and the pilgrims remained orderly, contented, and peaceful. They took Gallipoli 2015 as it was given; respected it for what it was, and didn't trash it for what it wasn't. The patient, well-behaved rank and file Aussies and Kiwis who came to be a part of something they truly believed and made us look good.

Lots of negative reports floated around in certain quarters about the heavy contingent of VIPs and bureaucrats in attendance. If they'd been fewer, it was said, the site would not have been so over-crowded. Fair enough.

I actually felt sorry for the night's fat cats. But arriving in comfort at 4 a.m. they missed the incredible camaraderie that existed in the Cove stands and the overcrowded grassy courts on that amazing night. They missed the togetherness and the bonding, the strong links of the common experience, and the invisible exchanges of emotion.

For every person who attended that gig, there would have been warm memories of past loved ones lighting up the darkness of their loss. Someone could have told the Canberra masterminds that in the great old days of the Circus World, the magic of the Big Top was all about treating everyone to the same intimate thrills at the same time in the same place, and in the same breath. And that's what happened at Anzac Cove.

Maybe the Turkish Government and its cohorts—the Governors of Çanakkale and Eceabat, back-handed the Commerative by not following through on the completion of road works, not making sure that the Turkish Food Vendors were able to deliver on the sites, and in not having the Eceabat-Anzac Cove tunnels ready. These blunders were ultimately upstaged by a mob of forthright ordinary folks who followed their own rules, and handed the Anzac Legend another reason to live for another hundred years.

Done deal, mate!

But allow me to make a point about the entire Commemorative epic.

Suppose the all-wise Canberra bureaucrats, who always think in arithmetic, had engaged the services of an events mastermind like David Atkins or Ric Birch, and turned a genius loose on the project. We may well have scored a spectacle that could have made the world sit up and sing. Okay, so it didn't happen, and okay, I suppose I'm just channelling Oliver Twist—a wishful kid, standing around with big hopeful eyes saying, *"Please sir, I want some more."*

That's a strictly personal opinion on my part. I have spent my life in the creative swirl of live theatre, television, singin' and dancin', newspapers and food, and I would have appreciated a Steven Spielberg take on the big night. What makes matters worse is that our house was robbed twice in 2001. My Personal Computers, printers, fax machines, telephones and television sets were taken, so were reference files that contained photographs and memorabilia relating to my father. None of those items were valuable, and none would have meant anything to anyone but me and my family. They would have been taken and tossed away after inspection. None were ever recovered. I downloaded the image of Dad in this book from an Internet file on the 5th Light Horse.

When I mentioned my wishes for a more fanciful Gallipoli 2015 to a friend who watched the telecast, he said:

> *"Overstatement would have been overkill. Its clout was in its simplicity. Everything that needed to be said was said. To be truthfully honest, that was one lily that didn't need to be gilded, because it was open to the interpretation that I wanted to put on it."*

I have come to the conclusion that he was right. The amazing thing was that Dad's diary wasn't taken. It was kept in a plain box that sat on a shelf beside some ordinary looking reference books.

I've often wondered about that. Sometime miracles can happen if you just leave them alone to surprise you.

AUTHOR BIOGRAPHY

MY EARLY LIFE WAS SPENT in live theatre: acting, direction, designing, writing. That led to a career in television: writing cop shows, panel games and soaps for Crawford Productions in Melbourne and Reg Grundy Productions in Sydney and Brisbane.

I partnered in one fine dining room and two theatre restaurants (Victorian melodrama and satirical revue... The Mark Twain and The Living Room Brisbane).

As a weekly columnist for the *Brisbane Courier-Mail*, *Brisbane Sun,* and *The Brisbane Sunday Mail*, I had a twenty-two-year second career writing lifestyles, food, theatre, fashion, entertainment and mainstream events (London, Paris, California, Hong Kong, Singapore, Kuala Lumpur, Hawaii, Finland, all Australian capitals). I do not write about people or places I haven't experienced. Currently freelancing.

Happily married to an amazing woman: two kids, three grandkids, one poodle.

INDEX OF IMAGES

MY FATHER: CHARLIE LORD ……………………………..9

CHARLIE LORD'S DIARY ……………………………….. 27

THE GALLIPOLI PENINSULA MAP …………………………. 53

BATTLESHIP BOUVET AND WINSTON CHURCHILL ………. 61

THE RIVER CLYDE ……………………………………….. 71

CAPE HELLES AND IAN HAMILTON …………………….. 131

ANZAC COVE AND WILLIAM BIRDWOOD ………………....... 158

THE 100 YEAR COMMEMORATIVE ………………………... 241

INDEX OF DIARY ENTRIES

MAY 5, 1915 49
MAY 6 50
MAY 7 50
MAY 8 50
MAY 9 51
MAY 10 77
MAY 11 77
MAY 12 82
MAY 13 82
MAY 14 85
MAY 15 86
MAY 16 86
MAY 17 87
MAY 18 87
MAY 19 87
MAY 20 90
MAY 21 90
MAY 22 90
MAY 23 91
MAY 24 92
MAY 25 94
MAY 26 95
MAY 27 98

MAY 28	99
MAY 29	99
MAY 30	100
MAY 31	100
JUNE 1	117
JUNE 2	117
JUNE 3	118
JUNE 4	118
JUNE 5	120
JUNE 6	125
JUNE 7	126
JUNE 8	133
JUNE 9	133
JUNE 10	133
JUNE 11	139
JUNE 12	139
JUNE 13	140
JUNE 14	140
JUNE 15	144
JUNE 16	146
JUNE 17	151
JUNE 18	152
JUNE 19	152
JUNE 20	152
JUNE 21	153
JUNE 22	154
JUNE 23	157
JUNE 24	157

JUNE 25	158
JUNE 26	158
JUNE 27	161
JUNE 28	162
JUNE 29	164
JUNE 30	164
JULY 1	166
JULY 2	167
JULY 3	168
JULY 4	168
JULY 5	171
JULY 6	171
JULY 7	171
JULY 8	172
JULY 9	172
JULY 10	172
JULY 11	173
JULY 12	173
JULY 13	175
JULY 14	175
JULY 15	176
JULY 16	176
JULY 17	176
JULY 18	177
JULY 19	177
JULY 20	177
JULY 21	177
JULY 22	177

JULY 23	177
JULY 24	178
JULY 25	178
JULY 26	179
JULY 27	179
JULY 28	181
JULY 29	181
JULY 30	181
JULY 31	181
AUGUST 1	181
AUGUST 2	182
AUGUST 3	182
AUGUST 4	186
AUGUST 5	187
AUGUST 6	187
AUGUST 7	191
AUGUST 8	193
AUGUST 9	193
AUGUST 10	194
AUGUST 11	194
AUGUST 12	194
AUGUST 13	197
AUGUST 14	198
AUGUST 15	198
AUGUST 16	199
AUGUST 17	201
AUGUST 18	202
AUGUST 19	202

AUGUST 20	202
AUGUST 22	202
AUGUST 22	203
AUGUST 23	203
AUGUST 24	203
AUGUST 25, 26, 27, 28, 29	204
AUGUST 30 and 31	204
SEPTEMBER 1	204
SEPTEMBER 2, 3, 4, 5, 6, 7, 8, 9	204
SEPTEMBER 15	205
SEPTEMBER 25	205

KENN LORD

www.ingramcontent.com/pod-product-compliance
Lightning Source LLC
Chambersburg PA
CBHW071728080526
44588CB00013B/1943